The Subtle Influence:

Conflicts of Interest in Financial Planning

FRANK C. BEARDEN, PhD.

iUniverse, Inc.
New York   Bloomington

The Subtle Influence:
Conflicts of Interest in Financial Planning

iUniverse books may be ordered through booksellers or by contacting:

iUniverse
1663 Liberty Drive
Bloomington, IN 47403
www.iuniverse.com
1-800-Authors (1-800-288-4677)

Because of the dynamic nature of the Internet, any Web addresses or links contained in this book may have changed since publication and may no longer be valid. The views expressed in this work are solely those of the author and do not necessarily reflect the views of the publisher, and the publisher hereby disclaims any responsibility for them.

ISBN: 978-1-4502-3338-5 (sc)
ISBN: 978-1-4502-3336-1 (ebook)
ISBN: 978-1-4502-3337-8 (hc)

Library of Congress Control Number: 2010907576

Printed in the United States of America

iUniverse rev. date: 8/20/2010

Contents

PREFACE

I have been concerned about conflicts of interest since becoming an insurance agent thirty-five years ago. Although I did not collect my thoughts on the subject until some years later, I was always uneasy about providing financial recommendations to someone with whom I had a valued, nonprofessional relationship. And yet, my early sales training encouraged soliciting insurance business from friends and relatives (as well as other sources). On the one hand, I cared more in some ways for such persons than for an unrelated prospect, and strongly wanted to help with their financial matters. On the other hand, I experienced difficulty forming and expressing my best thoughts about the individual's financial circumstances. I always felt the other relationship I had with the individual was at risk, so I often "pulled my punches" with recommendations to keep the other relationship in tact. In the end I concluded that I just could not do my best work with these conflicted relationships. The conflict provided too much negative impact on my quality of work, with the client being the ultimate loser.

This book is an effort to make a summary statement about conflicts of interest within a very special context and one I strongly care about, financial planning. My career in financial services and planning coincides with much of the historic development of financial planning as a profession, and I have identified with the efforts of those who set the quality bar high for this new profession. From that viewpoint, I have always viewed conflicts of interest as a deterrent to good practice that should be faced and remedied. Acting on that viewpoint is the motivation for this book. As a beginning contribution, I dedicated the research for my Ph.D. degree to this subject, exploring the perception of conflict that financial planners experience when considering an engagement with a close relative.

The concepts and applications of this book have come from a blend of four sources. My scholarly reflections have been collected in financial planning and advisory publications such as the *Journal of Financial Planning, Financial Planning Perspectives Audio Series* (CE courses, College for Financial Planning), *Financial Planning, Journal of Financial Service Professionals* (and predecessors), *Journal of Financial Counseling and Planning,* and *Advisor Today* (and predecessors). My work endeavors until two years ago contributed 32 years of involvement as a financial planner, advisor, and supporter of financial planners and advisors with the practitioners of Thrivent Financial for Lutherans, Prudential, MetLife, and a number of independent firms. In addition, I have been fortunate to have had many fruitful and pertinent conversations with academics dedicated to financial planning education, especially some of the faculty in the College for Financial Planning and The American College. These experiences have gelled the thoughts expressed here and solidified my conviction that the subject of conflicts of interest in financial planning practice should be fully developed. Last, but certainly not least in influence has been the scholarly influence of the Leadership faculty of Our Lady of the Lake University in contributing to my current understanding of conflicts of interest.

Among the many persons who contributed to the development of my thinking are a few individuals that should be mentioned. Dr. Malcolm Ree, the chair of my doctoral dissertation at Our Lady of the Lake University, San Antonio, Texas, and Dr. Mark Green, a member of my committee, helped me to accept that conflicts of interest are a problem with any profession, and as financial planning is a profession (even if a new one), they are a problem here also. Dr. Jesse Arman, Vice President of Academic Affairs for the College for Financial Planning provided a peer-review of this material, making substantive recommendations and offering encouragement for the project. The contributions of all are appreciated; the responsibility for the final work product is mine alone.

The material in Chapter 8 was first published in a CE course for the College for Financial Planning audio series *2009 Financial Planning Perspectives*, entitled "Conflicts of Interest Originating within a Financial Planning Practice," and is used here with permission. The administrative offices of the College are in Greenwood Village, Colorado.

INTRODUCTION: ARE CONFLICTS OF INTEREST A BIG DEAL?

CHAPTER 1

Conflicts of Interest in General

As this introduction is being written in early June of 2009, the United States is slowly emerging from what has been termed by Jack Healy in the *New York Times* as "the worst financial crisis since the Great Depression" (Healy, June 4, 2009). The analytical work as to the reasons for the crisis is still in process, but some of the broad contributing factors are assumed to be the issuance of large numbers of subprime mortgages, the drop in housing prices, defaults and foreclosures of the mortgages, and the run on capital for commercial and investment banks and other large financial institutions, not necessarily in that order. Because a significant part of the damage can be attributed to the general subject of this book (Strier, 2008), the event seems an appropriate place to begin a discussion of conflicts of interest. What follows is a discussion of some of the more significant factors at work in what occurred, to uncover the subtle role played by a major conflict of interest.

The Subprime Mortgage Crisis
Sold and resold.

In the recent past, subprime mortgages in the U.S. began being issued on a large scale to persons with low credit scores, little credit history, or other credit impairments. In 1996, $96.8 billion of subprime mortgages were originated and in 2006 the total rose to approximately $600 billion (Coval, Jurek, & Stafford, 2009). The issuing organizations of subprime mortgages sold these loans to investment banking firms to receive fresh capital to lend again. The investment bankers then structured these loans Into what can be loosely categorized as collateralized debt obligations or CDOs, to sell to institutional investors such as commercial and investment banks, hedge funds, pension plans, and insurance companies. The investment banks sought ratings on credit quality by credit rating services such as Moody's, Standard & Poors, and Fitch to facilitate the sales. The rating services were paid for their work by the investment bankers. The rating services also regularly provided these CDOs with high level, investment grade ratings that reflected little default risk, similar to the ratings for high quality bonds (Strier, 2008). Between 2005 and 2007, approximately 80 percent of the subprime mortgages were in CDOs given AAA ratings (Kim, 2008).

In fact, the subprime mortgages that were a major part of the collateral in the CDOs were of low credit quality (Coval, Jurek, & Stafford, 2009). The default rate for CDOs with investment grade ratings was significantly higher than that for similar ratings given to corporate bonds. Corporate bonds receiving Moody's lowest investment grade rating of Baa between 1983 and 2005 had a default rate over 5 year periods of 2.2 percent, while CDOs for the same period defaulted at a rate of 24 percent (Calomiris & Mason, August 24, 2007).

Highly rated CDOs had a distinct advantage over similarly rated bonds in that they had higher rates of return (David & Goldstein, June 18, 2007) which was a primary reason for their popularity. In 2006 the issuance of CDOs in the United States was $312 billion, a 102 percent increase from 2005, also a record year (Thompson, Callahan, O'Toole, & Rajendra, 2007). Had the CDOs been rated as somewhat speculative, their placement with institutional investors would have been on a much lower scale.

As CDOs grew in popularity, the revenue generated by credit rating services in their work with investment bankers grew significantly. Moody's revenue for the fourth quarter of 2007 rose 86 percent, and revenue for the year rose 24 percent. CDOs accounted for 44 percent of the revenue (Strier, 2008). In addition, credit rating organizations also provided consulting services to the investment bankers for the CDOs they later rated. These services included how to structure the debt products to receive higher ratings. Consulting on CDO type products accounted for 40 percent of Moody's revenue in 2006 (Levitt, Sept. 7, 2007).

Frank C. Bearden, PhD.

Defaults begin.

With CDOs backed by subprime mortgages in place on a large scale in the portfolios of large commercial and investment banks, insurance companies, and hedge funds, the subprime mortgages began to default. The defaults occurred due to the interaction of a few distinct factors. A good place to begin reviewing these factors is with the characteristics of subprime loans. The structure of subprime loans was a major contributor to rising defaults. The majority of subprime mortgages originated from 2003-2007 were designed with a fixed rate of interest for two or three years and then an adjustable rate tied to a measure of market interest rates. These were known as short-term hybrids. Typically interest rates rose two or more percentage points after the initial period. Through mid-year of 2008, delinquencies on adjustable-rate mortgages rose to over 29 percent, while fixed-rate mortgage rates rose to 9 percent (Mayer, Pence, & Sherlund, 2009).

Lowered standards of credit worthiness also were a significant contributor to defaults. Median loan-to-value ratios increased from 90 percent in 2003 to 100 percent for originations in 2005 and 2007. Subprime loans with a second lien increased from 7 percent in 2003 to 28 percent in 2006. Subprime loans with the highest loan-to-value ratios at origination from 2005-2007 had the highest rates of default. Loans with little or no documentation of income or assets also contributed to the rising default rate. These subprime loans increased from 32 percent of the subprime loans originated in 2003 to 38 percent in 2007. From 2003 to 2008 serious delinquencies of subprime loans with little or no documentation rose from 5 percent to over

25 percent, while fully documented loans rose from 5 percent to approximately 20 percent (Mayer, Pence, & Sherlund, 2009).

The combination of subprime mortgages structured with adjustable rates and lowered credit worthy standards produced a loan portfolio with inherent vulnerability to changes in the larger economy. Two such economic changes that brought out this vulnerability in the loans were the price of housing and mortgage interest rates. Prior to 2005, increases in housing prices, low rates of interest and low unemployment encouraged the growth of subprime lending. In 2005, the increase in housing prices began to slow. By 2007, housing prices were actually in decline in areas of the United States, falling an average annual rate of 10 percent from mid-2006 until mid-2008 (Mayer, Pence, & Sherlund, 2009).

Falling housing prices had the following effects on mortgage holders: The subprime mortgagors who put little or no down payment on their homes, incurred negative equity with falling prices. So when they had financial difficulties, they may have opted for default as their only choice (Foote, Gerardi, and Willen, 2008; Gerardi, Lehnert, Sherlund, and Willen, forthcoming; Sherlund, 2008). Owners with positive equity had an additional choice when encountering financial difficulty. They were more likely to refinance or sell their homes than go through default and foreclosure. Even if the mortgagor could not afford the mortgage, selling the house was more profitable than foreclosure (Mayer, Pence, & Sherlund, 2009).

Upward interest rate movement provided the catalyst for the defaults described above. Interest rates were low in 2003 until mid-2004, rising almost 2 percent from then until mid-2006, as measured by the London Interbank Offered Rate

(LIBOR). A fully indexed rate in a subprime mortgage would have increased from 8 to 11.5 percent. This translated to a 25 percent increase for a mortgagor whose two or three year level rate changed to an adjustable rate. The mortgagor would have experienced an approximately $250.00 payment increase on a loan of $150,000. This level of increase could and apparently did produce financial difficulty for many mortgage holders (Mayer, Pence, & Sherlund, 2009).

The vulnerability of subprime loans due to structure and lowered creditworthy standards positioned this debt as operable only in optimal conditions. The changes brought by dropping housing prices and rising interest rates interacted with the vulnerability to produce historically high default rates (Mayer, Pence, & Sherlund, 2009).

And the markets responded.

The market value of CDOs began to drop due to growing subprime defaults and commercial banks were soon seeking large sums of capital to restore their capital requirements. Investment banks also suffered, as Lehman Brothers declared bankruptcy, Bear Stearns was sold to Morgan Stanley, and Merrill Lynch was sold to Bank of America. The federal government approved $700 billion in the Troubled Assets Relief Program to help failing commercial banks and other large financial institutions (Lengell, March 30, 2009).

A key factor in these events was the high credit ratings given to the CDOs by the credit rating services, reflecting investments with low default risk and higher returns than other investments of the same rating. This encouraged the impressive scope of the issuance and purchase of CDOs. The credit ratings given to these investments were a *direct function* of the professional judgment of the credit rating agencies. That judgment was *flawed*, as evidenced by the default experience of CDOs compared with the default experience of other similarly rated debt instruments such as corporate bonds (Calomiris & Mason, August 24, 2007). The flawed judgment occurred *concurrently* with significantly increased revenues from CDO rating and consulting business by the credit rating services, which leads to the conclusion that a relationship existed between the two (Strier, 2008). The credit rating agencies had a conflict of interest with their investment bank clients that impaired the raters' professional judgment. The flawed judgment could well have arisen from reduced objectivity due to the prospect of additional revenues. Had the resultant ratings of the credit ratings reflected the true speculative nature of the investments involved, their appeal would have been much less and the incidence of these CDOs in institutional investor accounts would have been much lower. The lower incidence would have lowered the impact of subprime defaults. In summary, a conflict of interest held by the credit rating agencies was a significant contributor to the current financial crisis (Strier, 2008).

Conflicts of Interest in Financial Planning

The prior few pages provide evidence of the importance of conflicts of interest *in general*, especially in light of the damage they can and will generate. This book is about conflicts of interest in the practice of financial planning, so we have to look elsewhere for evidence of the importance of the issue within this context. In reviewing the financial planning landscape, we will consider some recent and not so recent statements about conflicts of interest in financial planning from a diverse group of credible sources: a respected financial planning credential granting organization, the largest financial planning professional organization and a sister organization, a state regulatory agency, the media, and a well-known financial planning professional.

First, let's consider two significant recent activities by the Certified Financial Planner Board of Standards. The *CFP Board's Standards of Professional Conduct* was adopted by the Certified Financial Planner Board of Standards to regulate the professional principles and behavior of all persons that are certified to use the CFP® mark. The *CFP Board's Standards of Professional Conduct* was revised May 31, 2007, took effect July 1, 2008, and was enforceable for CFP® professionals January 1, 2009. Within the *CFP Board's Standards of Professional Conduct* the "Code of Ethics and Professional Responsibility" establishes the principles and standards of practice (CFP Board, 2009, p. 6). Principle 4 is entitled "Fairness" and has a clear stipulation regarding conflicts of interest: "Fairness: Be fair and reasonable in all professional relationships. Disclose conflicts of interest" (CFP Board, 2009, p. 6).

The "Rules of Conduct" section (within *CFP Board's Standards of Professional Conduct*) specifies professional behavior required to uphold the principles and standards of the "Code of Ethics and Professional Responsibility." Rule 2 addresses "Information Disclosed to Prospective Clients and Clients" (CFP Board, 2009, p. 8), and Rule 2.2b stipulates that a CFP® certificant must disclose:

A general summary of likely conflicts of interest between the client and the certificant, the certificant's employer or any affiliates or third parties, including, but not limited to, information about any familial, contractual or agency relationship of the certificant or the certificant's employer that has a potential to materially affect the relationship. (CFP Board, 2009, p. 10)

In conjunction with the revision of the *CFP Board's Standards of Professional Conduct,* with provisions directly addressing conflicts of interest, the CFP Board of Standards has been actively promoting the use of the fiduciary standard for all financial professionals who offer broad-based financial advice. On December 8, 2008, the CFP board, the Financial Planning Association®, and the National Association of Personal Financial Advisors announced joint involvement in the Financial Planning Coalition, seeking regulatory reform through legislation to assure that financial planning services are provided with fiduciary accountability and transparency (CFP Board, Public Policy and Advocacy section, 2009, para. 1-3). Among the principle concerns by the CFP Board and Financial Planning Coalition is the necessity that pending legislation adequately addresses measures to regulate conflicts of interest among those providing financial planning services (CFP Board, letter to House Committee on Financial Services, November 2, 2009).

A third milestone event occurred on March 20, 2007, underscoring again the importance of conflicts of interest within financial planning. The United States Court of Appeals for the District of Columbia granted the petition of the Financial Planning

Association (FPA) in their lawsuit against the Securities and Exchange Commission. The SEC's final rule exempting broker-dealers from the requirements of the Investment Advisors Act of 1940 was overturned. The FPA contended that a professional who functions as a registered investment advisor—RIA, or an RIA representative—must be subject to the Advisors Act, and two provisions in particular: putting clients first using the fiduciary standard of service, and disclosing conflicts of interest prior to accepting an engagement (FPA, 2007). The FPA filed this suit, in part, because many financial planners provide investment advice and are RIAs or RIA representatives (Churchill, 2007).

Going back a little further in time, on March 2, 2006, the Financial Planning Association of Australia (FPA Australia) announced the adoption of the FPA principles to manage conflicts of interest. The principles are part of the FPA Australia's ongoing efforts to help members achieve high professional standards and effectively manage conflicts of interest (FPA Australia, 2006).

The emphasis on disclosing conflicts of interest by the CFP Board and the emphasis placed on conflicts of interest in recent actions by the FPA and the FPA Australia underscore their significance in financial planning practice. Now let's consider an incident involving a state regulatory agency described in the *New Hampshire Bureau of Securities Regulations*, July 12, 2005. The state securities regulators settled a complaint against a major financial planning firm regarding inadequately disclosed conflicts of interest. The Bureau charged that the planning firm had failed to properly warn clients of material conflicts of interest including higher commissions on firm-managed mutual funds than similarly styled and performing funds available from unaffiliated money managers. The planning firm settled, agreeing to a large fine and restitution to any harmed investors; in addition, the firm agreed to retain an independent consultant to review practices related to the use of proprietary mutual funds (*New Hampshire Securities Regulation*, July 12, 2005).

Next, to get an early view of conflicts of interest from the popular financial press, consider the title of an article by Ruth Simon in *Money* magazine back in November of 1992, entitled "The Broken Promise of Financial Planning: Conflicts of interest, incompetence and outright fraud lurk in many parts of the financial planning industry. Here's how you can keep from becoming a casualty" (*Simon,* Nov. 1992). Without judging the merits of Ms. Simon's article, we must admit that she and *Money* magazine perceived a market for the article's issue among readers.

Finally, consider the remarks of a well known and respected financial planner and writer, the late Lynn Hopewell, CFP. In his column "The Practice" in the *Journal of Financial Planning,* October of 1989, entitled "Conflicts of Interest: A Profession Maturing" Hopewell stated:

> We should start by developing a master catalog of conflicts of interest. Then we should issue interpretative memoranda that grapple with practical situations and problems, and illustrate principles using case examples. With experience and ethics enforcement, our list will become longer and the interpretations will become more elaborate and more sophisticated. (p. 163)

Hopewell closed with a forecast: "We will become a profession only after we behave like one. Better handling of our conflicts-of-interest will improve our behavior" (p. 163).

The recent actions by the CFP Board and actions of two major financial planning associations, combined with the incident involving a state securities regulator, an early commentary by a popular financial magazine, and a column by a well-respected financial planning professional twenty years ago provide compelling evidence that conflicts of interest have been and are a significant issue in financial planning practice.

As in the experience of the credit rating agencies, the influence of conflicts of interest in financial planning is subtle but dangerous. If not recognized and remedied, the bad professional judgment from a conflict of interest will damage a client's financial plan and a financial planner's reputation. Like the experience of the credit raters, the influence of a conflict of interest is usually recognized *after* its damage has been done.

Limited Experience with Conflicts of Interest by Financial Planners

Professionals in professions much older than financial planning, such as law, have had extensive experience with conflicts of interest. This is largely because their work product has been available for professional and public scrutiny for a much longer period than that of financial planners. While there is some disagreement as to the date of the beginning of the legal profession, the practice of law is thought to have been established by the beginning of the 4th century (Jones, 1964).

Financial planning, in contrast, is a much younger profession, varying in age with the authority used. According to Brandon and Welch in their book *The History of Financial Planning* the profession began with the meeting in Chicago on December 13, 1969 of the newly formed Society of Financial Counseling Ethics. This organization created the International College for Financial Counseling, renamed as the College for Financial Planning, and the CFP® certification was introduced in 1972 (2009). On the other hand, Duane Thompson has made the point that financial planning can be viewed as originating with investing counseling, which developed early 1920s and culminated with the formation of the Investment Counsel Association of America in 1937(Thompson, 2002). Robert Crowe, a former professor of financial and insurance at The American College, stated the first financial services practitioners who claimed to be financial planners appeared in the late 1960s (1993).

Longer exposure of professional work product, such as transcripts of court cases and legal documents, gave attorneys a longer period to scrutinize their work product for improvements. Where flaws were noted, as they are in all professions, the longer history of the legal profession provided attorneys more opportunities than financial planners to seek out the reasons for poor workmanship. The legal profession has come to recognize conflicts of interest as a significant contributor to damaged work products. As a reflection of this awareness, the *Model Rules of Professional Conduct* of the American Bar Association (ABA) has 11 specific rules that treat conflicts of interest with current clients alone (ABA, 2008).

In contrast, the financial planning professional associations, while also recognizing the importance of conflicts of interest, do not contain nearly as much treatment of the issue. The Financial Planning Association *Code of Ethics* treats the subject with one rule (FPA, 2009). The National Association of Financial Advisors (*NAPFA*) *Code of Ethics* has one rule about conflicts of interest (NAPFA, 2009). The Society of Financial Services Professionals *Code of Professional Responsibility* provides one rule and three applications (SFSP, 2008). Financial planners who are CPAs with the Personal Financial Specialist certification (PFS) are somewhat of an exception, due largely to their position within the Certified Public Accounting profession, itself over 100 years old (Flesher, Miranti, & Previts, 1996). The AICPA/PFS *Statement of Responsibilities in Personal Financial Planning Practice* is not available for non-member viewing (AICPA/PFS, 2009), but Rule 102 in the AICPA *Code of Professional Conduct* (AICPA, 2009) provides nine examples of possible conflicts of interest.

The point is not that attorneys are more diligent in their treatment of conflicts of interest than financial planners. In fact, the professions are quite different, which certainly accounts for some of the difference in the extent of discussion in the codes of ethics. The primary point is simply that attorneys have had *much more time* to recognize the nature of conflicts of interest and the kind of damage they can cause to professional practice. As reflected in their codes of ethics and professional conduct, financial planners through professional associations such as the FPA, the NAPFA, the SFSP, and the AICPA/PFS have done significant initial digestion of the implications of conflicts of interest in various areas of practice (FPA, 2009; NAPFA, 2009; SFSP, 2008; AICPA/PFS, 2009). This book is written to contribute to that effort. My intent is to look closely at the nature of conflicts of interest as they occur in financial planning practice, to reflect the "feel" of this dysfunction in its financial planning variations.

Summary

Conflicts of interest *are* a big deal with serious repercussions. The current financial crisis has shown us this. Conflicts of interest in financial planning are also a big deal, as reflected by the practice directives of the CFP Board, the efforts of the Financial Planning Coalition to insure fiduciary accountability for all who provide financial planning services, the legal victory of the FPA against the SEC, and other earlier events and pronouncements by a financial planning organization of another country, a state regulatory organization, a member of the popular financial press, and a dignitary in the profession. So now we know we have an issue.

What's Ahead

The flow of chapters goes like this: Chapter 2 shows the experience of a financial planner who yields to the influence of an interest competing with his client interest and the difficulties that result. The experience is a fictional composite of many factual situations I have encountered. My intent here is not to explain, but just to describe how the process of succumbing to a serious conflict can easily occur. Chapter 3 will carefully consider what happened in the experience, so the implications of each key aspect of the developing conflict can be seen and considered. Chapter 4 focuses on naming the problem, providing the history and a description of the nature of conflicts of interest. Chapter 4 closes with the question of why financial planners should care.

Chapter 5 examines the area of conflicts that are not conflicts of interest. The volume and speed of information today produces no shortage of conflicting moments. Is each of these a conflict of interest? After clearly establishing what a conflict of interest is and is not, Chapter 6 examines the appearance of a conflict of interest as seen by someone other than the financial planner. This phenomenon is sometimes known as a perceived conflict of interest. The chapter establishes why a financial planner should take the appearance of a conflict of interest as seen by others seriously. Chapters 7 and 8 review where conflicts of interest are likely to originate in a financial planning practice. These are areas where a practicing planner is likely to have or develop strong interests that run counter to the planner's interest in a client. Chapter 7 considers conflicts originating outside of financial planning practice and Chapter 8 describes those originating within practice.

Chapter 9 discusses the ways a conflict of interest can be recognized, advocating the method that generates the least damage to client and planner. Chapter 10 reviews remedies that maintain the client's best interest. Chapter 11 suggests a policy statement about conflicts of interest should be added to a planning firm's code of practice. The statement is a testimony to clients and prospective clients that the firm will not allow conflicts of interest to interfere with a client's best interest.

The approach of this book is essentially inductive, meaning it moves from a specific situation to a theoretical understanding of the situation or from fact to theory, in researcher language.

In contrast, the deductive approach moves from a theoretical understanding of similar situations to a specific situation or from theory to fact. We will use this method of understanding also, but most of the discussion will go from example to implications of the example.

In the book I will make liberal use of examples of financial planners, either as a beginning point as in Chapter 2 or to illustrate a conceptual point in later chapters. These examples are composites of my experience and study in financial planning and adjacent areas. Persons who know me may recognize references to parts of the country where I have visited or lived. All examples are based in fact, though the individuals are fictional. My intent with the examples is to bring the point I am trying to make as close to the reader's experience as possible. In the next chapter we will proceed to our primary example and the starting point of the discussion.

What Registered? An Assessment for Chapter 1

As a final note in this chapter you are now given the opportunity to test your distinguishing abilities through the concepts and applications of Chapter 1.

Please read through the following questions from the Introduction, asking if they are true or not and why? Educators call this an assessment (Suskie, 2009).

Question # 1 - T or F

The CDOs that included subprime mortgages were an appealing investment product to banks because they appeared to be an attractive combination of a safe investment with a higher return than other similarly rated investments.

Question # 2 - T or F

The conflict of interest that produced a highly rated CDO was the credit rating agency's self-interest of prospective increased revenue from providing the conservative rating for a high yielding investment. This interest conflicted with the credit rater's duty to the issuer of the CDO to rate the investment solely on its investment merits.

Question # 3 - T or F

Subprime mortgages developed historically high default rates due to low creditworthiness and an adjustable rate structure, combined with falling housing prices and rising interest rates.

Question # 4 - T or F

Principle 4 within the revision of the CFP Board's "Code of Ethics and Professional Responsibility" does not require disclosure of conflicts of interest.

Question # 5 - T or F

Professions much older than financial planning, like law, have had less experience with conflicts of interest than newer professions like financial planning.

The Answers and Why

Question # 1 - T or F

The CDOs that included subprime mortgages were an appealing investment product to banks because they appeared to be an attractive combination of a safe investment with a higher return than other similarly rated investments.

True. The CDOs with subprime mortgages posed the appearance of a strong advantage over other similarly rated investments, as the return of the CDOs was much higher (David & Goldstein, 2007). Thus the CDOs were attractive to financial organizations that required conservative investments, such as banks and insurance companies.

Question # 2 - T or F

The conflict of interest that produced a highly rated CDO was the credit rating agency's self-interest of prospective increased revenue from providing the conservative rating for a high yielding investment. This interest conflicted with the credit rater's duty to the issuer of the CDO to rate the investment solely on its investment merits.

True. The credit raters had the conflict of potential increased business and thus revenue from the issuers of the CDOs when providing conservative ratings, as the conservative ratings (combined with high potential returns) made the CDOs easier for the issuing firm to sell to institutional end-users such as insurers and banks. The influence of potential increased revenue conflicted with the professional obligation of the credit raters to the issuers of CDOs to rate the investments solely on their investment merits.

Question # 3 - T or F

Subprime mortgages developed historically high default rates due to low creditworthiness and an adjustable rate structure, combined with falling housing prices and rising interest rates.

True. Low creditworthiness means the mortgagor had a high loan to value ratio with little equity and little or no verification of income and assets. This made the mortgagor vulnerable to economic difficulties like losing a job or a rising loan payment due to an increased interest rate. The adjustable interest rates began to rise, and the mortgagor could not borrow from home equity, as there was little or none, especially when housing prices began to drop. With little verification of income or assets, the mortgagor may have been barely able to afford the house payment before it began to rise. Default was the result of many subprime loans.

Question # 4 - T or F

Principle 4 within the revision of the CFP Board's "Code of Ethics and Professional Responsibility" does not require disclosure of conflicts of interest.

False. Principle 4 in the CFP Board's "Code of Ethics and Professional Responsibility states: "Fairness: Be fair and reasonable in all professional relationships. Disclose conflicts of interest" (CFP Board, http://www.cfp.net/2009, ¶ 5).

Question # 5 - T or F

Professions much older than financial planning, like law, have had less experience with conflicts of interest than newer professions like financial planning.

False. Older professions like law have had *more* experience with conflicts of interest than younger professions like financial planning, as the work product of legal professionals has been available for review and scrutiny by professionals, clients, and the public for a long period of time than that of financial planners.

SERVING UP DAMAGE TO PROFESSIONAL JUDGMENT

CHAPTER 2

Background

Maurice Wills, CFP is a financial planner in Tulsa, Oklahoma. A few years ago a client of his named Mark Swinson, a successful commercial real estate broker and investor, offered Maurice a 25 percent share in a building in a suburb that he was about to purchase. Mark had access to attractive financing and had prepared a cash flow analysis showing anticipated profitability during the first year of ownership. Maurice was persuaded and became a joint owner in the building with Mark.

Today Maurice is anticipating a lunch with Mark. He and his wife Jean are significant clients for Maurice in terms of the trust they have in Maurice and the amount of fee revenue they provide him each year. This lunch is not to discuss the client's financial planning, but to discuss the mutual real estate venture Mark and Maurice had in the suburban office building. They meet once a quarter to review Mark's summary of the financial results of the building for the most recent quarter and the year to date. Today was such a meeting, made more significant because the previous quarter marked the end of another completed year. Mark emailed the performance documents to Maurice for his review before the meeting.

The year was a good one for the building, with a low vacancy rate and limited maintenance expense. Operating income for Maurice's share of the ownership came to almost $75,000. In addition, Mark provided a current valuation of the building, considering peer properties in the area. The building from the time of the purchase seven years ago to the present had appreciated at a rate of 10 percent per year.

The Meeting

Lunch went about as Maurice expected, except that Mark noted they should expect to make a significant investment in the building's electrical system in the next month or two, according to the building superintendent. Mark had estimates for the work and they had sufficient funds in their reserve account if no big surprises resulted. Towards the end of the meeting, Mark told Maurice he needed to make a revision in his financial plan as he had recently separated from his wife. While Mark stated he sincerely hoped they would reconcile, he wanted to cash in his life insurance that named his wife as beneficiary. He and his wife also were insured by a survivorship policy purchased earlier and owned by an irrevocable life insurance trust. He stated he was content to leave that policy as is for the present, intending to review it in the near future. The survivorship policy was to fund any estate expense at the second death and provide their one adult son with a significant inheritance. Mark wanted to surrender the policies he purchased more recently and owned personally.

Maurice was completely surprised, as the two couples had dinner together just a few months earlier and Mark and Jean seemed quite happy together. Maurice had the presence of mind to tell his client he would call him after reviewing Mark's file, to see what was involved. This satisfied Mark, who simply stated, "That's fine, but don't bother to mount a counter consideration for me, as you usually do, because I'm set to do this."

Further Reflection

Back in his office, as he reviewed Mark and Jean's financial planning file, Maurice noticed what he thought he remembered about the policies. The life insurance policies in which Jean was beneficiary were purchased over five years ago and were intended to provide her with $500,000 of cash for transition purposes for three years from the date of Maurice's death. The policy premiums were funded by quarterly income Mark received from an inheritance from his grandfather. The inheritance had remained in Mark's ownership alone since his grandfather's death. By design, the policies were no load, variable universal life contracts with strong cash value accumulation. The policies provided the benefits of satisfying the couple's interest in additional tax-deferred funds and funding a transition period for Jean.

Maurice believed he had two questions to consider regarding Mark's request. First, in light of what he was told by his client, was cash surrendering these policies a good idea? Second, if a change was indicated, what information, if any, should he communicate to Jean? After all, she was also his client. Underneath these questions was the fact that Mark was now responsible for a significant portion of Maurice's income. So what were the issues in each question?

"Well," Maurice thought, "if Mark was telling me the truth and he still hopes for reconciliation, then surrendering the policies seems like a bad idea. Kind of a knee jerk reaction. And even if he's not hoping to save his marriage, he should be told the factors to consider in doing this."

"And what about his health? I really don't know much about Mark's current health. Has it changed much since I recommended he apply for the second of those two policies? The policies are each over two years old, so contestability has expired. Death benefits can't be questioned except for fraud. There's a lot to think about!"

Maurice decided to make a checklist of the issues pro and con, to aid his decision of how to present the implications of cashing out the policies to his clients. As a source for his checklist, Maurice retrieved among other resources his insurance and estate planning textbooks from his graduate studies at the College for Financial Planning. He carefully began to find and highlight all pertinent discussions, marking each comment with a large paper clip.

Maurice had a harder time figuring out the disclosure owned to Mark's wife Jean. On the one hand, Oklahoma was not a community property state, and because the policies were funded with separate property from their inception, Maurice reasoned Mark owned all the cash value of the policies. However, their financial planning was done together, involving otherwise completely commingled assets and active consideration for each other. And Mark wanted this service completed while they were clients as a couple. Surely this meant Jean should at least be told if the policies were to be surrendered. In fact, she should be a party to the discussion, he thought. Maurice even wondered if he could continue to serve both Mark and Jean if the separation continued or ended in divorce, because of the obvious conflicts he would have in serving each party. The more he thought about it, Maurice wondered how he could be a party to a decision for one client that might not be in the best interests of another client, the first client's wife. After all, he would not enter a client relationship that would be adversarial to an existing client.

To switch his concentration for a few minutes, Maurice took another look at the performance figures on the building. Even with the additional expense coming up, the building had been more profitable than Mark originally estimated. As a final diversionary thought, Maurice recalled that he and Mark spoke at their last quarterly meeting of investing in another building when Mark could find a suitable property.

The Decision

Even though Mark indicated in his last comment that he was not in a mood for "complete disclosure" from his financial planner, Maurice decided to dedicate an hour to considering the issues about cash surrendering the policies. For simplicity, he would separate the issue of the cash surrendering the policies from considerations involving Jean. He constructed the following chart to organize his thoughts:

Points Favoring Cash Surrender:	Counter Arguments:
Client wants to do so.	May be a premature decision, in light of possible reconciliation of the marriage. Also the policies are past the contestable period for death benefits (Introduction to Life Insurance, 2009, p. 62).
The policies are owned by client.	Yes, but they were purchased for Jean and the children's benefits.
Policies remain separate property as Jean has no incidence of ownership (Leimberg & Doyle, 2004, p. 459).	Some of cash values could be taxable (Tax Facts, 2009, Q. 250, p. 292).
Beneficiary is not irrevocable, so Mark can change at will.	No counter argument
Office can facilitate cash surrender.	No counter argument
Mark's estate has sufficient liquidity for Jean with current valuations of securities.	Jean would have sufficient, but not surplus liquidity during the 3 year period, based on current securities valuations.

Points Favoring Disclosure to Jean	Counter Arguments:
Jean is a joint financial planning client with Mark and should be a party to any material changes in their financial plan.	Mark owns the policies and does not want the cash surrender disclosed to his wife.
Jean is a client and I have a fiduciary responsibility to her to act in her best interest and do her no harm. She should be involved in this decision.	Discussing this with Mark could cause me to lose him as a client. This could affect my part of the real estate ownership because Mark has controlling interest in the building. Also, he has the expertise and interest to find another property for our investment.
Perhaps the best course is to reevaluate the client relationships so each interest can be treated fairly. Maybe another planner or planners should be involved.	Mark would disagree, this course would eliminate the pre-divorce advantage he appears to be seeking over his wife. I would lose him as a client, my investment in the real estate venture would be at risk.

With the chart in hand and reviewed, he decided to recommend that his client hold off surrendering the policies until the direction of his marriage became clear. When this insight was available, Mark could revisit the issue, carefully considering all relevant points, including the welfare of Jean and their three children. Maurice would recommend that this discussion be made with Jean's participation or he would have to reconsider their financial planning relationships.

At this point, Maurice called Mark. Maurice's opening question was why Mark wanted to surrender the policies. Mark replied that he felt the coverage really wasn't needed with his other assets and he had a use for the cash values. Mark went on to state he did not want his wife Jean to know about the surrender. Maurice stated he felt she should be involved in this decision under his obligation as her financial planner. Mark then curtly stated:

"These policies are my property, they always have been, she has no rights to them, and I can do what I please without notifying her or anyone else! If you don't want to proceed this way, I can find another financial planner to assist me."

"Will cashing out the policies still seem a good idea to you if your separation ends and your marriage continues?" Maurice asked.

"Of course, Maurice, that really has nothing to do with this request."

Maurice's best judgment was to recommend that Mark holds off cash surrendering the policies until he was certain about the direction of his marriage. The assets would be available in the insurance policies for a later surrender, if desired then, and the growth in the cash values *was* tax-deferred. However, he sensed that his resistance to cashing in the policies angered Maurice and he did not want a significant part of his own cash flow from their building jeopardized in any way. So he decided to instruct his employee in charge of product procurement and service to do what was needed to process Mark's request. He also decided not to contact Jean regarding the cash surrenders or separating the client relationships between her and Mark.

"I will instruct our financial product specialist to gather the appropriate forms for your signature. Should I ask him to call you at your office for a brief appointment to complete these?"

"That will be fine," Mark responded. "And please do not contact Jean about this."

"Done," Maurice replied, and the conversation ended.

The Aftermath

Wednesday of the following week Mark came in to complete and sign the forms to surrender the life insurance policies. He met with Maurice briefly, completed the forms, and was out of the office in 15 minutes. The forms were faxed and mailed to the insurance company, to speed processing time. The company was instructed to send the checks directly to Mark at his office address.

Several months later the Swinsons filed for divorce. Jean sent Mark a letter terminating their financial planning agreement. A few weeks later, Maurice received notice of a lawsuit Jean filed against him for breach of contract, claiming he failed to uphold his fiduciary responsibility by failing to make her party to or notify her of Maurice's intent to cash surrender the policies. She attached a note stating she planned to file a complaint with the CFP Board (CFP Board, 2009). This produced some apprehension in Maurice's mind. He had to admit he felt uneasy because he did not hold to his professional opinion or make his opinion a matter of record with his client. In addition, if Jean filed a complaint against Maurice to the CFP Board, he could face disciplinary action.

Maurice and Mark maintained their real estate relationship, later purchasing a second building. Maurice remained Mark's financial planner. Only now Maurice's recommendations seem more like Mark's recommendations. He has come to care less about the integrity and distinction of his practice and more about his real estate investments.

Summary

In this chapter we have watched a financial planner make important professional decisions because of an outside business venture with a client. In Chapter 3 we will get some inductive mental exercise by looking closer at what occurred in this incident, to form an understanding of the key factors that produced the outcome.

What Registered? An Assessment of Chapter 2

Now you are given the opportunity to test your distinguishing abilities through the concepts and applications of Chapter 2. Please read through the following questions from the chapter, asking if they are true or not and why?

Question # 1 – T or F

Maurice and Mark shared the real estate venture before Mark and his wife Jean formed a financial planning relationship with Maurice.

Question # 2 – T or F

Maurice finally agreed with his client Mark and processed the cash surrenders of the life insurance policies because he felt Mark's wife Jean did not need the benefits of the insurance.

Question # 3 – T or F

The policies Mark wanted to cash surrender listed Jean as beneficiary and were intended to fund a three year transition period after Mark's death.

Question # 4 - T or F

The interest Maurice had that exerted strong conflicting influence against his best professional judgment on behalf of his clients Mark and Jean was the relationship from their joint real estate venture.

Question # 5 – T or F

Maurice faced an initial financial downturn because of his decision to facilitate surrendering the life insurance policies for Mark.

The Answers and Why

Question # 1 – T or F

Maurice and Mark shared the real estate venture before Mark and his wife Jean formed a financial planning relationship with Maurice.

False. Mark and his wife Jean had the financial planning relationship with Maurice first and then Mark and Maurice became joint investors in the real estate venture.

Question # 2 – T or F

Maurice finally agreed with his client Mark and processed the cash surrenders of the life insurance policies because he felt Mark's wife Jean did not need the benefits of the insurance.

False. Maurice finally agreed with his client Mark because he wanted to protect his interest in the joint real estate venture he shared with Mark.

Question # 3 – T or F

The policies Mark wanted to cash surrender listed Jean as beneficiary and were intended to fund a three year transition period after Mark's death.

True. The survivorship policy was owned by an irrevocable life insurance trust and was intended to pay estate expenses at the second death of Jean or Mark.

Question # 4 - T or F

The interest Maurice had that exerted strong conflicting influence against his best professional judgment on behalf of his clients Mark and Jean was the relationship from their joint real estate venture.

True. The real estate venture was a success and making a significant contribution to Maurice's income. Mark had mentioned the prospect of investing in another property, and Maurice did not want to put this relationship at risk. When faced with choosing his own best professional judgment or protecting the real estate relationship by doing what his client requested, Maurice sacrificed his judgment.

Question # 5 – T or F

Maurice faced an initial financial downturn because of his decision to facilitate surrendering the life insurance policies for Mark.

False. We are not told of any initial financial downturn. Mark and Maurice continued their financial planning and real estate relationships, buying another building. Maurice did lose Jean as a client and is facing litigation from her and a possible complaint to the CFP Board. His biggest downturn may be the drop in his valuing of his professional integrity and the distinction of his financial planning practice.

WHAT HAPPENED?

CHAPTER 3

The experience Maurice had, as described in Chapter 1, is a common one for financial planners to this extent: most decisions regarding a client involve a *number* of factors to consider. A financial planner has responsibility to diligently review the issues pertinent to the decision, evaluate these by priority, and make the decision. In the process of deliberation, factors frequently enter the planner's line of thought that are *unrelated* to the financial planning service provided by the planner, but are important to the financial planner for other reasons. In this chapter we will expand on the facts of the incident to get a good understanding of the underlying factors that moved the financial planner to make the decision he made.

The Financial Planner's Initial Position

The boundaries of Maurice's best professional viewpoint and judgment about the issue of surrendering the insurance policies can be seen in the initial conclusions he reached, just before calling his client after their lunch. He decided his client's desire to cash surrender the life insurance policies was premature and should be postponed until the future of his marriage was clear. When the future of the marriage was apparent, the client could revisit the issue with active participation from his wife Jean. In Maurice's initial position, if Mark was unwilling to do this, Maurice would require that the three parties reconsider their financial planning relationships.

Maurice's initial viewpoint concerned only factors clearly pertinent to the financial planning relationships: the life insurance policies, their current purposes for the family, Mark's desires to put them to another use and Jean's right to be involved. While Maurice had an active interest in his part of the real estate venture, this was *not* part of his first considerations regarding Mark and Jean. At that point, he viewed the real estate venture as an important *outside* issue. Maurice's judgment as to what Mark should do was developed from his professional viewpoint and informed *only* by information *directly pertinent* to the clients' financial planning.

The Change in Viewpoint

To understand the change in Maurice's actions in this scenario we have to consider when his thinking changed and why. Then we should examine his subsequent actions and the work product that resulted from his change in viewpoint. As noted above, Maurice initially did not view his involvement in the real estate venture as a financial planning consideration for his clients. The matrix he formed to consider the cash surrenders shows this, for there is *no mention* the real estate venture through this part of the matrix.

The first hint of a change in his view occurred when he began to think about his fiduciary responsibility to Jean. At this point he mentioned the real estate venture for the first time in the *Counter Arguments* column. Something about involving her in the decision brought about an association with his personal stake in the venture with Mark. Perhaps he realized that insisting on her involvement would bring significant resistance from Mark and *that* could negatively influence his real estate investment. *From this point on*, Maurice considered his investment as a significant factor in the financial planning for Mark and Jean. Thus Maurice's professional viewpoint toward his clients now became *distorted* to include an investment concern of his own, of equal or higher weight than the financial planning relationship. His real estate investment was now within the boundaries of his financial planning perspective for his clients.

The Change in Viewpoint Leads to a Change in Judgment

A financial planner's professional judgment involves the interaction of the financial planner's professional *viewpoint* with new financial planning information of the client. In other words, professional judgment is the application of the planner's professional viewpoint (perspective) to new planning pertinent data to reach a conclusion in service to a client. This application involves the financial planner interpreting the client's information in light of client goals and objectives, and often involves providing recommendations. So when a financial planner's professional point of view about a client becomes heavily weighted with the inclusion of the planner's *own* interests (thus distorted), the planner's resulting professional judgment will be weighted in a similar fashion. And that is exactly what occurred: Maurice exercised poor professional judgment in deciding he would instruct his employee to process Mark's request for the cash surrender values. He also exercised poor judgment in not insisting on Jean's involvement in the decisions, so her interests could be fairly addressed.

Work Product Follows

At this point, we should notice that what appeared to be a mere nuisance conflict for the financial planner now can be seen to be a much more serious conflict, with greater influence that damaged the financial planner's professional judgment. When a financial planner's professional viewpoint and judgment on behalf of a client are distorted by an interest not pertinent to the client's financial planning, the resulting work product (written, verbal or otherwise) for the client will be distorted as well.

Distinguishing a financial planner's professional judgment from work product is difficult, because work product is based on and results from judgment. A financial planner's professional judgment becomes work product *when it is communicated to a client as the planner's opinion, advice or recommendation.* Maurice provided distorted work product when he stated his intent, which implied his opinion, to expedite the cash surrender process and not contact Jean, an involved client, about the matter.

Who Gained or Lost?
The clients.

What did clients Mark and Jean gain or lose from their financial planner's distorted judgment and work product? Let's consider Mark first. No one can deny that he got what he requested. Maurice arranged for the policies to be submitted for cash surrender over his client's signature and said nothing to Mark's wife Jean. So Mark received the cash proceeds without Jean's knowledge and used them for his purposes.

What did he lose? First Mark lost the objective advice of his financial planner. Objective advice is a form of professional work product and means providing advice that takes all pertinent facts into account and is free from influence outside of the professional issues of the client. Principle 2 within the *Code of Ethics and Professional Responsibility* of the *CFP Board's Standards of Professional Conduct* requires a CFP certificant to maintain objectivity in service to a client (CFP Board, 2009, p. 6). The financial planner in this situation traded his objective advice for distorted advice that served his own interest. Had Maurice maintained his original position, his client would have been encouraged to consider a more thorough assessment and an appropriate recommendation. That is not to say the client would have agreed with and acted on the appropriate recommendation.

Second, by acting on Maurice's position, Mark clearly took steps against his wife's financial interest and without her knowledge. These two actions negatively affected any remaining personal relationship he and his wife shared. So by acting with Maurice's agreement, Mark lost some of the credibility he may have had with his wife. His actions also may have reduced his bargaining position in the divorce proceedings.

What about Jean? What did she gain? She appears to have received no benefit from the actions of her financial planner. What did she lose? We do not know if Jane learned about the cash surrenders at the time of the processing. If she did not know of the surrenders at the time, she would not have known how her husband acted against her interests. Even without this knowledge, Jean clearly lost the coverage on her husband's life. The survivorship policy was in an irrevocable insurance trust and provided little direct benefit to Jean at Mark's death. Whenever she learned of her husband's actions, Jean lost at least some of the trust she may have had in him. Because Maurice did not honor his fiduciary relationship to her, Jean also lost trust in her financial planner.

The financial planner.

What did the financial planner gain? Well, he maintained the financial planning engagement with Mark. He also gained the ability to continue his real estate venture with his client, which led to another building and possibly increased financial prosperity. So Maurice gained on the top line.

What did he lose? Although he acted in a manner his client Mark wanted, he may have lost some of Mark's respect, as Maurice was influenced to approve of a procedure that deceived another of his clients. He certainly lost the trust and respect of Jean, as well as some of his peace of mind due to her suit against him. Maurice may face some sanction from the CFP Board. More important than these losses, Maurice lost some of the integrity of his practice, and with this, his interest in distinguishing the quality of his professional service.

Summary

In this chapter we determined that Maurice Wills gave up his professional opinion as a result of a powerful financial conflict. He contributed to his client's deception of his spouse, another client. He also prospered financially. In the process Maurice failed to perform his fiduciary duty to serve in the client's best interest for either client, in order to attend to his own interest. The organization Fiduciary *360* in its fiduciary handbook *Prudent Practices for Investment Stewards* warns against the kind of decision Maurice made, stating: "Fiduciaries and parties in interest are not involved in self-dealing" (p. 19). Maurice lost his relationship with one of the clients and encountered a lawsuit with the client who severed the financial planning relationship. Finally Maurice faced professional sanction and came to lose interest in the integrity and distinction of his financial planning practice. In Chapter 3 we will take a closer look at the type of a conflict Maurice faced and how such a conflict develops. Then we will focus on why financial planners should be concerned about these types of conflicts. In a later chapter we will review remedies for such conflicts and show how a financial planner can turn these damaging influences into a practice-enhancing characteristic of quality financial planning.

What Registered? An Assessment of Chapter 3

Now you have the opportunity to test your distinguishing abilities through the concepts and applications of Chapter 3. Please read through the following questions from the chapter, forming short answers that best respond to what is asked.

Question # 1

What was the financial planner's initial position about his client Mark's request and when was it formed?

Question # 2

What additional factor entered the financial planner's consideration about his client's request that came to change his decision about what he would do in response to the request?

Question # 3

What was the financial planner's work product in this example?

Question # 4

What did the client Mark gain and lose in this example?

Question # 5

What did the client Jean gain and lose in this example?

Question # 6

What did the financial planner gain and lose in this example?

The Answers and Why

Question # 1

What was the financial planner's initial position about his client Mark's request and when was it formed?

The financial planner initially decided his client's desire to cash surrender the life insurance policies was premature and should be postponed until the future of the marriage was clear. When the future of the marriage was apparent, the client could revisit the issue, with active participation from his wife Jean. If his client was unwilling to do this, Maurice should require that the three parties reconsider their financial planning relationships. The financial planner in this example reached his initial position just before calling his client after their lunch appointment.

Question # 2

What additional factor entered the financial planner's consideration about his client's request that came to change his decision about what he would do in response to the request?

Maurice the financial planner came to include his involvement in the real estate venture as a pertinent factor in his thinking, which changed his decision about his course of action.

Question # 3

What was the financial planner's work product in this example?

The financial planner's work product was his stated intent to expedite the cash surrender process and not make Jean, an involved client, aware of the matter. In stating his intent, he implied his opinion that the process was a good idea. A financial planner's professional judgment becomes work product when communicated to the client as the financial planner's opinion, advice or recommendation, whether written or not.

Question # 4

What did the client Mark gain in this example?

Mark gained the cash proceeds of the insurance policies without Jean's knowledge. He lost the objective advice of his financial planner and credibility with his wife.

Question # 5

What did the client Jean gain and lose in this example?

She does not appear to have gained anything from the actions of her financial planner. She lost the insurance coverage on her husband's life. When she learned of her husband's actions, Jean lost some of the trust she may have had in him. Jean also lost trust in her financial planner.

Question # 6

What did the financial planner gain and lose in this example?

He gained the ability to maintain the financial planning engagement with Mark. He also gained the ability to continue his real estate venture, which led to another building and possibly increased financial prosperity. He may have lost some of his client Mark's respect, as approved a procedure that deceived another of his clients. He lost the trust and respect of Jean, and perhaps some peace of mind due to her suit against him.

He may lose some of his good standing with the CFP Board. Most important, he lost some of the integrity of his practice and his interest in distinguishing the quality of his professional service.

NAMING THE PROBLEM

CHAPTER 4

In the last chapter we described the underlying factors that influenced a financial planner to give up his professional opinion for a powerful conflicting interest. In this chapter, we will name and describe the type of conflict the financial planner experienced in Chapter 2. Once we've done this, we will review how this particular kind of conflict develops. We then will consider a brief history of professional judgment, a concept that is essential for understanding the type of conflict reflected in Chapter 2 and the subject of this book. We will then review the history of this type of conflict, concluding the chapter by taking a focused view of why financial planners should care about such conflicts in the practice.

A Special Kind of Conflict

Because the conflict experienced by the financial planner in Chapter 2 did not go away, but competed with interest in the client to the point of distorting the planner's professional judgment in service to a client, the conflict is a special type known as a *conflict of interest* (Davis, 2001). From the scenario, what can we conclude about conflicts of interest? The first fact we know is a conflict of interest is an interest a financial planner has *in addition to* professional interest in a client. Second, the additional interest cannot become a conflict of interest unless it is an interest that concerns the financial planner *when in practice.* Up to this point, the additional conflict is just an interest the financial planner has in addition to professional interest in the client, and generates no conflict with the planner's professional judgment. In the example in Chapter 2, the additional interest was a real estate investment.

Third, we know from the scenario that a conflict of interest *draws time and focus away* from the planner's professional interest in the client. We could say the conflict of interest *competes* with the financial planner's professional interest for time with and focus on the client (Davis, 2001).

These three characteristics will pose no serious problem to the client relationship of the financial planner if the financial planner can manage the competing influence of the additional interest like any other competing interest. With *most* competing interests, the financial planner can simply repress the interest and continue to provide quality professional service to the client, perhaps dealing with the distracting interest at another more appropriate time, or not dealing with it at all.

But a conflict of interest is not easy to repress and dismiss. This type of conflict is different from other competing interests in two ways. A conflict of interest has *much stronger* influence than a common competing interest. A conflict of interest is simply *too* strong to repress and reconsider at another time or ignore completely. The example in Chapter 2 shows that the conflict of interest "reappeared" as the financial planner attempted to analyze the issues involved in making a recommendation to his client. A conflict of interest *will not leave* the financial planner's awareness when the planner attempts to dismiss it. This is the fourth characteristic of a conflict of interest.

The strength of influence of a conflict of interest can be understood knowing that conflicts of interest frequently appeal to our self-interest and thus generate an automatic, visceral, often unconscious response. This type of influence will take precedent over an influence that requires a controlled response (Moore & Loewenstein, 2004).

The fifth characteristic of a conflict of interest develops from the fourth and is the most important: A conflict of interest will *damage* the financial planner's professional judgment. The damage begins when the conflict of interest distorts the planner's view of the client relationship. The damage continues when the distorted viewpoint leads to distorted judgment on behalf of the client. In the example in Chapter 2 the distorted judgment was the financial planner's decision to support the changes in his client's life insurance policies that directly affected the client's wife, also a client, without first discussing the changes with her.

The last two characteristics of a *stronger influence* and *damage to professional judgment* mean a financial planner cannot deal with a conflict of interest like any other competing interest. If the planner attempts to do so, the conflict of interest will gain the financial planner's attention at the expense of client interest and will damage the planner's judgment on behalf of the client. With the serious implications conflicts of interest pose, we might now consider how they develop.

How do they develop?

Conflicts of interest develop like any other competing interest. For interests outside of practice, a conflict of interest can arise from an existing client relationship when the financial planner and client discover they share *another* interest outside of the client relationship. The additional interest then grows into such a strong influence that it becomes a conflict of interest. That's what happened in the example in Chapter 1. Maurice had a client relationship with Mark prior to forming a business interest with him involving a commercial property.

As stated earlier, most competing interests do not rise to the level of being or becoming conflicts of interest, so most of the interests a financial planner shares with clients will not develop into a conflict of interest. As a second path in which conflicts of interest develop from an interest outside of practice, the financial planner may have a nonprofessional interest with an individual *first* and *then* consider forming a client relationship with the person(s) involved. The prior relationship will become a conflict of interest for the newly formed business relationship if the prior relationship impairs the professional judgment of the financial planner on behalf of the new client. This second type of development has been fairly common in financial planning, due to some of the origins of financial planning in the marketing of insurance products, which emphasized prospecting for clients among existing friends and business associates (Huebner &

Black, 1982). Conflicts of interest outside of practice will be more thoroughly discussed in Chapter 7.

Finally, a conflict of interest can develop within a financial planning practice, when an interest a financial planner has in providing service to a client becomes corrupted by self-interest and competes with the planner's professional judgment. The interests that can become corrupted include the roles the financial planner plays in providing service to clients, as well as the client relationships themselves. Conflicts of interest within financial planning practice will be considered in detail in Chapter 8. This is a good point to consider a brief history of the concept conflict of interest. However, because the concept conflict of interest developed from the concept of professional judgment, we will first review how professional judgment developed within a short history of professions.

A brief history of professions.

The growth of the importance of professional judgment was a necessary prior development before the origination of the concept conflict of interest. We defined professional judgment in financial planning in Chapter 2 as ". . . the application of the planner's professional viewpoint (perspective) to new planning pertinent data to reach a conclusion in service to a client" (p. 22). Professional judgment is an outgrowth of the development of professions from occupations. Professions as we know them did not exist before medieval times. Prior to this time, professional work was done by persons serving in other capacities, such as physicians who were also slaves of wealthy Roman households (Roos, 1992).

During the medieval period of 1200-1450, medicine, law, and the clergy developed into what we know as professions. By the end of the eighteenth century, these three groupings gained independence from religious control by organizing professional associations. In the 19th century, other occupations such as dentistry, architecture, and engineering began to professionalize, forecasting the creation of additional professions in the future (Roos, 1992).

The contemporary criterion of a profession, according to a theory known as trait theory, includes five characteristics. First, a profession possesses knowledge and skills that distinguish its members from nonmembers. Second, due to unique expertise, members of a profession are able to exercise autonomy in performing service. In fact, professional codes of ethics allow professionals to regulate their own conduct. Third, professional knowledge allows members of a profession to claim some authority over clients, patients, or students. Fourth, professions are viewed as service-oriented rather than profit-oriented. Finally, an occupation acquires the status of a profession when the public recognizes it as such (Hodson & Sullivan, 1990).

The specialized knowledge of professionals, combined with the increasingly brief interaction of individuals with professionals in free-market economies, contributed to the growth of the *authority* of professionals. Individuals receiving service from professionals became unable to evaluate the judgment of professionals and came to rely instead upon a *relationship of trust* (Davis, 2001). At this point professional judgment became very important precisely because those receiving the judgment were unable to evaluate it and had to rely on the professional. Professionals came to be viewed as persons upon whom an individual was dependent for service. With that dependence, the independence of the professional became important. Davis noted the reason for this: ". . . we do not want ordinary self-interest to guide the decisions of those on whom we depend; instead, we want those on whom we depend to be 'independent,' 'impartial,' or the like" (p. 4).

As the authority of professions grew, the responsibility of a professional to a client or patient grew in recognized importance, and a professional's relationship with a client or patient became highly valued. The highly valued (and ultimately fiduciary) relationship and the importance of the professional's independence raised the importance of the professional's judgment rendered on behalf of the client. Conflicts of interest were and are a threat to that independent judgment.

Then conflicts of interest.

The term conflict of interest is a concept about half-century-old. It first appeared in the unabridged Stein's *Random House Dictionary of the English Language* in 1971 (Stein, 1971) and gained entry into *Black's Law Dictionary* in 1979 (Black, 1979). The first court case to use the term conflict of interest was probably in 1949. However, the development that preceded and brought about the use of the term conflict of interest began much earlier (Davis, 2001).

Probable the first profession to recognize the issue of conflicts of interest was the legal profession. As we referenced, perhaps the earliest recorded example of this conclusion involved attorneys in the bankruptcy proceeding of the Equitable Office Building Corporation in New York, 1949. According to the bankruptcy judge, an attorney was considered to have a clear conflict of interest if the attorney agreed to represent a creditor in the bankruptcy proceeding while at the same time trading in the securities of the company in bankruptcy, without prior permission from the court. Furthermore, the bankruptcy judge stated that an attorney who did this should be refused a legal fee for representing the creditor. An attorney was thought unable to perform quality representation, including rendering professional judgment for the plaintiff while engaged in investing in the securities of the defendant in the same litigation (*Equitable Office Bldg. Corp.*, 1949).

In 1969, the *ABA Code of Professional Responsibility* defined a conflict of interest as the dilution of the attorney's loyalty to a client (ABA Code, 1969). Because of the importance of professional judgment for professionals, a conflict of interest came to be seen as a type of *early warning signal* of a significant problem that the professional *could not entertain* and honor rightful duty to the client. In 2001, Michael Davis, a renowned ethics scholar defined a conflict of interest as an interest a professional has in addition to a professional relationship that tends to interfere with "the proper exercise of judgment" in the professional relationship (Davis, p. 8). Following the legal profession, other professions, including financial planners and advisors, began to recognize the impact that conflicts of interest imposed upon relationships with clients and came to address conflicts of interest in their codes of practice (AMA, 2009; APA, 2009; AICPA, 2009; CFP Board, 2009; SFSP, 2009).

Frank C. Bearden, PhD.

Why Should Planners Care?

Why should financial planners be concerned with conflicts of interest? We can begin to answer this question by recalling the role a conflict of interest played in the "the worst financial crisis since the Great Depression" (Healy, 2009). Conflicts of interest left unaddressed can generate high stakes consequences. From that general point, we can look to the implications of a conflict of interest in financial planning. Let's view matters first from the *client's experience*, using the episode in Chapter 2 as an example. By supporting his client's actions, Maurice contributed to the client's deceptive actions regarding his wife. We do not know how influential this experience was to her view of her husband, but we can assume the event was not seen as a positive occurrence. The planner made a negative contribution to the relationship of two then married persons, a contribution the client's wife (also a client) had to digest.

Second, although her husband did not die during the example, had he died after the cash surrenders, his wife would have lost $500,000 of death benefits from the policies. In fact, this loss may still occur if she outlives her now ex-husband. In an article proposing reforms to protect clients from abusive financial planners, John Gray concluded that financial planner *self-interest* and incompetence are the two most widespread sources of money lost through bad advice incurred by planning clients (Gray, 1994).

Third, the client's wife also had a client relationship with the financial planner because she and her husband were served as a couple (Rattiner, 2006). Hence, she was faced with the fact that the financial planner did not honor his fiduciary responsibility to her. Now we can see three needless disappointments the financial planner provided to one client by being swayed by his conflict of interest with another client, the first client's then husband. A fourth client loss was supporting the husband's unethical behavior.

No client's experience is typical, so we cannot rightly conclude that this kind of client disappointment and loss will reoccur with each conflict of interest. What we can conclude is a conflict of interest left unarrested will likely provide client disappointment and loss of some kind.

What happened to the financial planner? Let's start with the fact that financial planners are paid for their advice. Because the conflict of interest damaged the judgment that informed the financial planner's professional advice, the advice itself was damaged. The financial planner's advice did not rise to standard of objective advice required in codes of practice such as the *CFP Code of Practice* (CFP Board, 2009) or the *AICPA/PFS Statement on Responsibilities in Personal Financial Planning Practice* (AICPA/PFS, 2009). Hopefully professional self-respect will motivate a financial planner to care about a conflict of interest for this reason first, because it will distort judgment and work product. The financial planner in the example in Chapter 2 realized ". . . he did not hold to his professional opinion or make his opinion a matter of record" (Chapter 2, p. 32). If a financial planner continues to ignore professional judgment due to a conflict of interest, the financial planner's confidence in his or her professional judgment will begin to drop due to lack of use. In addition, the planner may face practical consequences.

The wife and client who was uninformed of the surrender of her husband's life insurance policies sued the financial planner for breach of contract. So the financial planner had to defend himself against legal action. If the financial planner had disclosed his conflict of interest with Mark to both clients, as recommended by Katherine Vessenes (1997), Jean Swinson would be been forewarned that the planner's professional judgment would be suspect.

In addition, she stated she would file a complaint with the CFP Board for unprofessional conduct. This could affect the financial planner's ability to use the CFP® mark (CFP Board, 2009). Finally, the injured client had not, but might file a complaint with appropriate federal and state regulatory authorities.

In addition to official complaints, a client like Jean Swinson will be no endorsement for the financial planner's practice. With the ease of communication across the internet, the world is getting smaller, especially for predominantly local or regionally focused enterprises like many financial planning firms. Each former client with a bad experience changes from being a potentially good source for new clients into a bad advertisement. The public is becoming informed about conflicts of interest (McCall, 2004), so if a financial planning firm develops a reputation for engaging in conflicts of interest, many potential clients will be inclined to go to competitors for unimpaired professional service.

Clients don't always sue a professional when they believe they have been treated unfairly, and they may not complain to the CFP Board or the regulatory authorities. Some prospective clients will not know a firm's reputation for entertaining conflicts of interest in practice before agreeing to a professional engagement. Even if these negative results do not come to pass, the financial planner who ignores a conflict of interest has to live with the knowledge of doing shoddy work for a client. That alone should be sufficient motivation to encourage the planner to carefully consider how to deal with conflicts of interest.

Summary

In this chapter we stated a conflict that impairs the professional judgment of a financial planner is a conflict of interest. We proceeded to describe conflicts of interest and did a brief survey of the history of the preceding concept of professional judgment and then the concept conflict of interest. We closed by responding to the question of why financial planners should care about conflicts of interest. In Chapter 5 we will review the type of conflicts most commonly experienced by financial planners, those that do not develop into conflicts of interest. These conflicts often will frustrate the planner, but do not threaten the planner's professional judgment in work with a client.

What Registered? An Assessment of Chapter 4

Now you have the opportunity to test your distinguishing abilities through the concepts and applications of Chapter 4. Please read through the following questions from the chapter, forming short answers that best respond to what is asked.

Question # 1

What is the key characteristic of a conflict of interest?

Question # 2

Should a strong outside interest of a financial planner that does not concern the planner in practice be considered a conflict of interest?

Question # 3

Why is professional judgment important to a client, patient or student?

Question # 4

Which profession probably first recognized the issue of conflicts of interest?

Question # 5

Why should financial planners care about conflicts of interest in practice?

The Answers and Why

Question # 1

What is the key characteristic of a conflict of interest?

The key characteristic of a conflict of interest is the ability of the conflict to distort the professional judgment of a financial planner.

Question # 2

Should a strong outside interest of a financial planner that does not concern the planner in practice be considered a conflict of interest?

No, because the interest is of no concern to the financial planner when providing professional judgment for clients. Consequently, the interest will not conflict with or damage the financial planner's professional judgment, a key requirement for a conflict of interest.

Question # 3

Why is professional judgment important to a client, patient or student?

Because clients, patients, and students have come to value and depend upon professional judgment for their well being in the area of the professional's competence.

Question # 4

Which profession probably first recognized the issue of conflicts of interest?

The legal profession in 1949.

Question # 5

Why should financial planners care about conflicts of interest in practice?

Because a conflict of interest left unaddressed will lead to poor work product, bringing significant negative experience to a client (s) and the financial planner.

Conflicts That Are Not Conflicts Of Interest

Chapter 5

This Chapter will address the conflicts financial planners face that are not conflicts of interest and will not develop into conflicts of interest. These conflicts compete with the financial planner's client interests just as do conflicts of interest, but they do not provide the level of influence to damage a financial planner's judgment (Davis, 2001). Here are a few examples.

A Personal Conflict

Sylvia Browning is a financial planner in New Mexico. She is completing her recommendations for a new client who desires more income from her investments. Sylvia is trying to decide whether to recommend an immediate annuity or reconfigure the client's investment portfolio to generate regular income. As she assumed before her analysis, the immediate annuity provides more income, but the portfolio provides access to principal as well as cash flow, at a lower amount than the annuity. Within that theme, she has variations of variable annuities that provide some of both benefits.

In addition, Sylvia has a frequent source of distraction within her practice. She is writing a book about financial planning practice that describes frequently occurring situations she has encountered when a client strongly resists her recommendations. In these instances she typically compromises her recommendation to a limited extent in the name of making some improvement in the client's financial plan. That is not the issue of her book. The focus of the book is her conviction that client resistance occurs in certain identifiable situations. Sylvia is interested in naming the situations in which a planner will likely encounter client disagreement. The book has become a distraction because in the middle of work for a client she often finds herself wondering if the situation will qualify as an example of client resistance for her book. At this moment she is thinking that her client can afford to take the investment portfolio arrangement and keep her capital. Just as she begins to form her recommendation, she finds herself distracted by the thought that the next meeting with her client will make a good example for her book. She can just sense that her client will disagree with her inclination towards the portfolio. At that moment she notes she is off track with her work and stops thinking about the book. She returns to her calm deliberation to create good choices for her client. In an hour she has completed the remainder of the financial plan, including recommendations.

Sylvia's upcoming book is a distraction and a conflict, but it is not a conflict of interest. Why? Because she can ignore the influence when necessary and continue her focus on a client, with no impairment of professional judgment. Let's look at a more typical example.

A Social Conflict

John Kazantzakis is a financial planner in Houston. He has just completed a financial plan for a client who is an acquaintance and was a fraternity brother in college. The client was a year behind John in school, and they did not know each other well prior to meeting for financial planning purposes ten years later. Now they and their spouses are friends and occasionally do things socially. Because of their friendship, John hesitates to bring up two significant problems in his client and wife's financial planning: First, they have claimed questionable deductions on their federal income tax return. Second, they have far too little life insurance in light of their debt and family obligations. John assumes the discussion of both issues will meet with hostility and possibly put the friendship at risk. Nonetheless he knows both problems can be resolved with frank discussion and the clients' corrective measures. With this guiding motivation, John subdues his concern for the friendship and has the appropriate discussion with the client couple.

Friendship can pose a conflict of interest for a financial planner if the friendship is important enough to the planner. In this case the financial planner was able to sufficiently reduce the competing influence of the friendship so he could maintain his professional judgment and provide appropriate advice to his clients. The influence of the concurrent friendship was a competing influence or a distraction, but not a conflict of interest. We should also remember that friendships that do not lead to a conflict of interest can also lead to more candid client discussions than would occur without the friendship.

A Family Conflict

A third competing interest that is not uncommon among financial planners with families can come from teenage or adult children. Roger Monson is a financial planner with a 17-year-old son who has recently begun to do poorly in high school. The son is discouraged and fearful he may not have good enough grades or test scores to get into college. At some point in each day Roger finds himself thinking about how his son is doing in school.

This morning he is preparing for an annual financial plan review with an elderly widower client who wants to make provisions for his grandsons through trusts. At nine fifteen his son calls him from the school. He tells Roger he just took a test he was not expecting and fears he may not have done well. With this news Roger shuts the file on his client, although he has limited time remaining to adequately prepare for his client's concerns. After an initial struggle as to what to do, Roger realizes he cannot resolve the issue at the present. Spending time preoccupied this way is not helpful to his son or his financial planning practice. On the other hand, maintaining the quality of his practice does benefit his clients and everyone in Roger's household. Roger quickly calls his son back on his cell phone and promises he and his wife will help their son address his concerns that evening. Then he calls his wife and they agree to listen to their son over dinner and try to help him face his issues.

At that point, Roger returns to inheritance planning for his client. He completes preparation for the annual review in an hour and a half, including a lengthy call to a trust attorney of his acquaintance. He is pleased with his summarization of issues and his judgment in making preliminary recommendations.

After completing his preparation he asks his partner to review his work for errors in judgment. Roger's partner finds typographical errors and a small area of disagreement, but no errors in judgment.

Situations involving family members are often of significant influence and can provide distraction from focus on a client. Sometimes the influence is sufficiently strong that it cannot be subdued and takes precedence over client concerns. In this example, the financial planner was able to subdue the influence of his concern, make provisions to deal with the issue later and continue his client work with the exercise of sound professional judgment. Because the influence of the competing interest could be subdued without impairing professional judgment, the influence was a distraction but not a conflict of interest.

A Professional Conflict

Ernesto Reyes is a financial planner in California who is beginning work on an MBA degree with an emphasis in leadership. His interest is the application of leadership to client development so he can better influence his clients to achieve their financial goals. He believes he has missed several opportunities to be more helpful with clients because he did not know how to provide more appropriate influence in certain situations. Tonight he will have his first class and his apprehension about the class is distracting him from returning a client phone call.

Ernesto's concern is with having been out of school for over ten years. He is fearful that he will have difficulty keeping up with the pace of the class, given his study skills have had little recent exercise. The phone call from his client Dr. Schwartz came at nine fifteen and it's currently ten fifteen. Dr. Schwartz indicated in his message that the call was important but not urgent. Ernesto feels he is losing his chance to respond promptly to his client by being lost in thoughts over the upcoming class.

At that point he shakes off his apprehension and quickly realizes he has always been a good student. Furthermore, he has accomplished virtually everything he has set out to do. So he decides he will do what's needed to do well in the class and dismisses the subject. He turns around to his credenza, picks up the phone and listens to Dr. Schwartz's message again. He then calls his client.

The desire to constantly improve is a strong motivation for many financial planners and further education or training is a means to that end. But further education can be a challenge that brings apprehension that the challenge will not be met. The day of Ernesto's first class is a likely time to feel some of the chill of cold feet. Because he was able to nullify his fears about the class and exercise good judgment in calling his client, Ernesto's preoccupation is a conflict but not a conflict of interest. His sound professional judgment prevailed.

A Financial Conflict

Monte Johns is facing financial difficulty for the first time in five years. The downturn in the economy seems to have trickled down to his clients, who are scheduling their annual reviews several months after they are due or not scheduling them at all. They are also using his product procurement service to evaluate and secure financial products less than in recent years. Until this year, 87 percent of his product recommendations, all no load and implemented with a fee, were secured by Monte's firm. Through the first six months of this year, he has had a 53 percent implementation rate. Frankly, his procurement service typically generates about 40 percent of his firm's revenues. Fewer scheduled annual reviews and product implementations each month has resulted in a 32 percent drop in revenue to this point.

Interestingly enough, his financial downturn has drawn Monte somewhat off task with a client who did schedule her annual review as it came due. Mrs. Watson is a wealthy widow who has a strong affinity for the university she attended. Two years ago she agreed to a charitable remainder trust arrangement Monte suggested benefiting the university and Mrs. Watson. She has been very satisfied with the plan and happy with the contribution her alma mater will ultimately receive. Monte hits upon an idea that could expand Mrs. Watson's giving to the university and generate more fee income at just the right time. He will recommend she make another gift of this sort, gifting an apartment unit she owns. Of course the real estate market is down so the market value of the apartments is about 20 percent less than two years ago. In addition, Mrs. Watson stated when the trust was implemented that she thought her gift to the trust more than settled her "obligation" to the university for her educational experience.

"So how can I persuade her to consider increasing her gifting when the real estate market is down, especially since her rental income from the management company is very steady, by her comments?" Monte begins to engage his analytical abilities to make the case for this recommendation, which is against his most important ethical tenant: to act in the client's best interest. This idea does not satisfy his client's interests, from all indicators he has considered. Finally he decides he will not do this. Instead, he will look for more viable ways to increase the revenue of his practice.

Monte was tempted by a downturn in revenue to attempt a remedy that was not aligned with his client's needs and desires. The competing interest was strong enough that the financial planner briefly considered violating his primary rule of practice. But the distraction was temporary and Monte overcame the distraction to regain and exercise good professional judgment. The distraction was definitely a competing interest, but not a conflict of interest, because the financial planner was able to overcome the influence and maintain his professional judgment.

Conclusion: A conflict-free practice?

We live in a time when rapidly increasing amounts of information arriving at an accelerating speed have raised the likelihood of conflicts in our personal and professional lives. Complexity is on the rise and this brings conflicts. The term multi-tasking assumes we have multiple responsibilities and that brings conflicts that we must understand, prioritize and resolve. As residents of the information age, financial planners face conflicting demands for their attention on a daily basis. There is no way a financial planner today can avoid the experience of conflicts.

Fortunately most of the conflicts a financial planner will experience are of the type discussed in this chapter. They can be sufficiently resisted or removed so the financial planner's professional judgment remains sound and effective. Maggie Jackson discusses methods to manage distractions in an interview in *Harvard Management Update* (2009). She recommends becoming intentional and controlling with attention span, hesitant to react to outside demands on attention, and remembering that an immediate issue may not be an important issue. According to Jackson a financial planner should decide where to place his or her focus.

The conflicts that persist in competing for a financial planner's interest in a client and cannot be resolved as Jackson suggests, as a mere distraction, are conflicts of interest that can damage a financial planner's judgment and resulting work product. Clarity in being able to distinguish between these two general types of conflicts is critical for a financial planner to maintain high quality in practice.

Summary

In this chapter we discussed the type of conflicts that are not conflicts of interest, lower tier conflicts that do not rise to the level of impairing professional judgment. These are the conflicts of every day life that require merely a refocus of attention and effort to overcome and maintain sound professional judgment. In the next chapter we will discuss the appearance of a conflict of interest, also known as a perceived conflict of interest, as seen from the view of an individual other than the financial planner.

What Registered? An Assessment of Chapter 5

Now you are given the opportunity to test your distinguishing abilities through the concepts and applications of Chapter 5. Please read through the following questions from the chapter, asking if they are true or not and why?

Question # 1 – T or F

The conflict in Sylvia Browning's life was not a conflict of interest because she was able to stop thinking about her book and return her focus to a client and develop sound recommendations for the client's consideration.

Question # 2 - T or F

John Kazantzakis has a conflict of interest with the friendship with his former fraternity brother and his client relationship because he hesitated to bring up two significant financial planning issues in his friend's financial profile.

Question # 3 - T or F

Conflicts that are not conflicts of interest will not provide significant distraction or frustration to a financial planner.

Question # 4 - T or F

If a financial planner avoids conflicts of interest, her or his financial planning practice will be largely conflict-free.

Question # 5 - T or F

Managing the distracting conflicts that do not rise to the level of a conflict of interest requires that a financial planner refocus attention and exert effort to overcome the distraction and maintain sound professional judgment.

The Answers and Why

Question # 1 – T or F

The conflict in Sylvia Browning's life was not a conflict of interest because she was able to stop thinking about her book and return her focus to a client and develop sound recommendations for the client's consideration.

True. If her book was a conflict of interest, Sylvia Browning would have subjected her best professional judgment to the dictates of the book, leaving the client recommendations to less than her best judgment.

Question # 2 - T or F

John Kazantzakis has a conflict of interest with the friendship with his former fraternity brother and his client relationship because he hesitated to bring up two significant financial planning issues in his friend's financial profile.

False. Although John did hesitate in his professional judgment due to the friendship, he returned to his best thoughts and had an appropriate discussion with his friend and spouse about the issues.

Question # 3 - T or F

Conflicts that are not conflicts of interest will not provide significant distraction or frustration to a financial planner.

False. Conflicts that are not conflicts of interest can generate distraction and frustration. They are not conflicts of interest because the financial planner is able to maintain the quality of his or her professional judgment in spite of distraction and frustration.

Question # 4 - T or F

If a financial planner avoids conflicts of interest, her or his financial planning practice will be largely conflict-free.

False. Avoiding serious conflicts that will impair judgment does not eliminate all the other distracting conflicts that occur in a financial planning practice. No one is able to completely avoid conflicts. In fact, conflicts often enlighten an individual to other points of view and are thus growth enhancing.

Question # 5 - T or F

Managing the distracting conflicts that do not rise to the level of a conflict of interest require that a financial planner refocus attention and exert effort to overcome the distraction and maintain sound professional judgment.

True. These efforts will enable a financial planner to keep the important resource of professional judgment at hand and in good order.

THE APPEARANCE OF A CONFLICT OF INTEREST

CHAPTER 6

The appearance of a conflict of interest, as viewed by an individual other than the financial planner, is important for two reasons. First, the perception may be correct and a remedy should be found for the conflict of interest. This experience can occur when a conflict of interest is at work with a financial planner, but the planner has not realized or admitted the fact (Davis, 2001). Let's consider an example of how this could happen.

An Appearance That Reflects a Real Conflict of Interest

Marsha Horowitz is a financial planner in Carbondale, Illinois. She agreed a few months ago to do a financial plan for her aunt, a lady who became a widow in the last year and received a sizeable life insurance benefit from her deceased husband. The aunt was very generous to Marsha and her sister when they were children and was an important part of their childhood. The aunt had no children and wanted to plan her estate for Marsha and her sister's children's education. Marsha was initially hesitant to work with her aunt and even suggested that the aunt work with her partner, Carol Wilkes. The aunt was hesitant to work with someone she did not know, and Marsha did not push the matter.

In her last meeting with her aunt, Marsha presented a financial plan that included an asset allocation for the investable funds her aunt held. Based on the aunt's risk tolerance and objectives, the portfolio was conservative, with a minority position in common stocks. Her aunt was resistant, wanting to take much more risk, referencing some of the large technology companies. Marsha told her aunt she would like to research a few of the aunt's suggestions, buying time to mull over what she considered an inappropriate idea.

In her weekly meeting with her partner to discuss current cases, she talked about the aunt's resistance to what Marsha believed was the appropriate recommendation for her assets. Carol affirmed the appropriateness of asset allocation and asked Marsha what she planned to do. Marsha replied that she was inclined to do what her aunt wanted and provide a statement for the aunt to sign stating the arrangement was against her best judgment.

Carol suggested an alternative strategy, essentially staying with Marsha's recommendation, but providing a small compromise with a highly rated large cap technology fund. She also suggested that Marsha allow her to consult on her aunt's financial plan, with the aunt's approval, as Marsha was on the brink of a conflict of interest. Marsha agreed, as she was uncomfortable with the investments her aunt requested.

Marsha probably suspected she was entertaining a conflict of interest in working with her aunt, but had not admitted the fact. Her partner's perception of the conflict of interest was correct, and her recommendation was appropriate under the circumstances. We will address remedies for conflicts of interest in Chapter 8.

The second reason the appearance of a conflict as viewed by another person is important, even if the conflict is imagined, is because of the practical consequences that can occur due to the other party's conviction. Individuals often act on their convictions even if ill founded. A financial planner who ignores another party's observation about a conflict of interest because the financial planner knows the observation is false may face the consequences of the party's viewpoint. For this reason all perceived conflicts of interest by others should be addressed and all appropriate measures taken to remove the appearance of the conflict of interest. Further, the party holding the conviction of the conflict of interest should be told of these efforts and an attempt made to satisfy the party that the conflict does not exist in fact. The following example shows how this could be done.

An Appearance That Reflects an Imagined Conflict Of Interest

Michael Stewart served on the board of a local homeless shelter for several years with his new client George Norris, the president of a large regional bank. In the course of their service together, George made an appointment with Michael to discuss his financial planning concerns. Michael agreed and a client relationship developed. After the next board meeting, George casually mentioned one of his financial planning concerns with the attorney serving as legal counsel for the charity. He also referenced that he engaged Michael to help him with resolutions.

The following morning the attorney called George to express his concern that the engagement could constitute a conflict of interest with Michael's work on the board. He expressed the same sentiment in a call to Michael. Michael assured the attorney that he would talk with George and get back with the attorney to discuss the matter further.

George spoke with Michael and stated he had no concern about the conflict, but did not want the attorney serving the charity to be concerned. At that point, Michael said he would speak at length with the attorney. He called the attorney and asked him to lunch. In the course of lunch Michael stated that he enjoyed working with the attorney for the shelter and valued his opinion. Michael asked the attorney's reasons for his perception. The attorney stated that he observed the significant contributions George and Michael made to the development of the shelter and thought a client relationship would conflict with the independent decision-making of both persons with board business. He also stated the board relationship would probably be a conflict with the financial planning client relationship.

Michael thanked the attorney for his compliment and stated his commitment to the work of the shelter. He also stated that he always considered existing relationships before entering a new client engagement, thinking about his ability to function in an independent and objective manner in both roles. He maintained no outside interests or client relationships that involved conflicts impairing his judgment or responsibility to the organization or client. He did not think the client relationship would impair his independent functioning on the board. He stated that if such a conflict were to develop in his work with the board or with George, he would speak with his client and recommend recusing himself from the engagement. Michael closed with the comment that he hoped his explanation satisfied the attorney's concerns.

The attorney stated he was impressed with Michael's sincerity and was satisfied for the present. However, he reiterated that the independent functioning of board members was one of his ongoing concerns. Michael shared the content of the conversation with his client George and decided to continue to serve both as his financial planner and fellow board member at the homeless shelter. The next morning Michael paused and wondered what he would have done if the attorney remained adamant about the conflict. Because of the high value Michael placed on his service on the board of the shelter, he decided that if the attorney for the board persisted with his opinion that a conflict of interest was present, he would have referred George to other financial planners. He could not comfortably continue to serve on the board with the attorney holding an adverse position and George subsequently concerned. We will discuss remedies for appearances of conflicts of interest in Chapter 9.

This hypothetical example is intended to point out that even when the financial planner is right in theory, the financial planner still has to address the practical aspect of the situation.

In this case, the practical aspect involved the attorney who was important to the charitable organization on whose board the planner served, and thus important to the financial planner. The attorney also was important to the financial planner's new client, who also served on the board. For these reasons, the attorney's opinion about the conflict of interest he perceived between the financial planner and his new client had to be addressed, and was. To have avoided addressing the attorney's remarks would have risked the financial planner's position in an organization he valued, and risked the new client engagement he also valued.

Summary

In this chapter we considered the subject of the appearance of a conflict of interest. We reviewed why the view of a conflict of interest by another person should always be taken seriously and addressed. In the next chapter we will discuss the first of two origins of conflicts of interest in a financial planning (or any professional) practice, those conflicts that originate outside of practice (Stark, 2001).

What Registered? An Assessment for Chapters 2 Through 6

As a final note in this chapter you are now given the opportunity to test your distinguishing abilities through the concepts and applications of Chapters 1 through 6. Major subjects discussed include conflicts that are conflicts of interest, conflicts that are not (distractions), and conflicts that appear to be a conflict of interest in the view of another person. Several conflict situations are presented below with the underlying question: "Is this a conflict of interest, a temporary distraction, or the appearance of a conflict of interest, and why?"

Situation # 1

A financial planner provides advice for fee compensation and products for commission compensation from product suppliers. Commissions are 85 percent of the financial planner's revenue. Advice always includes the recommendation for new financial products with commissions.

Situation # 2

A financial planner serves on the board of an organization and makes a proposal for the organization's benefits program that involves the financial planner receiving commission and fee compensation.

Situation # 3

A partner in a financial planning firm is convinced one of the associates has a conflict of interest in recently forming an engagement with her sister. She has spoken to the associate, but the associate does not agree with her view of the issue.

Situation # 4

A client is a financial planner's close friend. In developing the client's financial plan, the planner recognizes a large life insurance need. The financial planner hesitates to make the recommendation due to his friend's expressed aversion to life insurance and anticipation that his friendship will be negatively affected. Nonetheless, he includes a well-founded life insurance recommendation within the financial plan.

Situation # 5

A client and a financial planner have a joint venture. The planner foregoes an important tax recommendation in the client's financial plan to maintain the business relationship.

Situation # 6

A financial planner has developed too many clients to continue making thorough annual reviews and has decided to reduce pertinent areas in the review process rather than hire additional professional staff.

The Answers and Why

Situation # 1

A financial planner provides advice for fee compensation and products for commission compensation from product suppliers. Commissions are 85 percent of the financial planner's revenue. Advice always includes the recommendation for new financial products with commissions.

This is likely a conflict of interest because the financial planner's advice *always* includes product additions. The financial planner's judgment appears to have compromised by the desire to always include additional financial products, which supports the financial planner's financial interest. This is an example of an internal conflict of interest in which the recommendation of remedies role played by the planner has become distorted into being more of a revenue generator than a means of professional service.

Situation # 2

A financial planner serves on board of an organization and makes a proposal for the organization's benefits program that involves the financial planner receiving commission and fee compensation.

This is a conflict of interest as fiduciary responsibility to the board significantly conflicts with the role of benefits provider. A board member has detailed knowledge of the organization's internal processes that will become an unethical advantage to a board member who recommends financial products and service for compensation to the board. This is an example of an outside conflict of interest due to the financial planner's relationship with an organization.

Situation # 3

A partner in a financial planning firm is convinced one of the associates has a conflict of interest in recently forming an engagement with her sister. She has spoken to the associate, but the associate does not agree with her view of the issue.

This is the appearance of a conflict of interest by another party, or what is often called a perceived conflict of interest. Whether these turn out to be true or not, they should always be investigated.

Situation # 4

A client is financial planner's close friend. In developing the client's financial plan, the planner recognizes a large life insurance need. The financial planner hesitates to make the recommendation due to his friend's expressed aversion to life insurance and anticipation that his friendship will be negatively affected. Nonetheless, he includes a well-founded life insurance recommendation within the financial plan.

This not a conflict of interest because the financial planner was able to maintain professional judgment and make the needed life insurance recommendation. This is a conflict that is a temporary distraction.

Situation # 5

A client and a financial planner have a joint venture. The planner foregoes an important tax recommendation in the client's financial plan to maintain the business relationship.

This is a conflict of interest because the financial planner compromised professional judgment to benefit the business venture. The situation is an example of an outside, financial conflict of interest.

Situation # 6

A financial planner has developed too many clients to continue making thorough annual reviews and has decided to reduce pertinent areas in the review process rather than hire additional professional staff.

This is likely a conflict of interest because the financial planner appears to have sacrificed sound professional judgment of maintaining the quality of annual reviews, perhaps by hiring additional professional staff, for reducing the quality of service provided with no additional expense. This is an example of an internal conflict of interest in which the financial planner's client relationships have become distorted, becoming more of a profit center than a professional practice.

CONFLICTS OF INTERESTS OUTSIDE OF PRACTICE

CHAPTER 7

The previous chapter discussed the perception of a conflict of interest by someone other than the financial planner. That chapter is important because some of the best insights about a possible conflict of interest in a financial planning practice come from other interested parties. In this chapter we will be begin examining where conflicts of interest *originate* in a financial planning practice. Conflicts of interest for a financial planner start in one of two places, from interests *outside* of practice or interests *within* the practice. Andrew Stark in *Conflict of Interest in the Professions* (Stark, 2001) calls these two origins *outside of* (professional) *role* and *within role* (p. 335-336).

Conflicts of interest arising outside of practice have had ample of discussion in academic and professional forums (Stark, 2001), but this area is still a matter of active discussion within financial planning, probably due to the relative newness of financial planning as a profession. For this reason, conflicts of interest from outside of practice are a good place to begin our discussion of where the conflicts *begin* for a planner. Conflicts of interest outside of practice can be separated into at least three categories: financial conflicts, personal conflicts, and conflicts arising from organizational responsibilities.

Financial Conflict of Interest

A financial conflict of interest outside of practice is an interest in which the financial planner stands to gain or lose financial assets (Bearden, 2002). The outside-of- practice financial interest may be ethical in its own right, like an outside source of income or an investment. The interest *becomes* unethical when it rises to the level of *damaging the financial planner's professional judgment.* The planner can become sufficiently *preoccupied* with the prospect of a gain or loss from an outside financial interest that he or she is unable to provide necessary *focus* and *conviction* to provide high quality professional *judgment* for a client. Financial conflicts also develop when a financial planner has a *joint* financial interest with a client. In this case, the planner's ability to form good judgment on a client's behalf is *hindered* by the financial planner's interest in the financial venture shared with the client. The outside of practice interest siphons off *energy* and *attention* required for the financial planner to think clearly about the client's situation.

An example.

Here is an example of an outside of practice conflict of interest of a financial nature: Mike is a financial planner in a large Midwestern city. He and his wife Jill own a successful property and casualty agency in which Jill is the primary agent. Two of the main products of the agency, automobile and homeowner coverage, are demand products for car and homeowners. Because Jill maintains contracts with insurance companies that provide very competitive auto and homeowner policies, the agency has prospered. In fact, the insurance agency has earned more than Mike's financial planning practice for the last three years. Mike functions as the business manager for the insurance agency.

Because of the growth of the agency, Mike has been spending three nights per week reviewing and preparing the books. Jill and Mike have discussed selling the agency in five years. Mike has become enamored with the agency because of the regularity of the income flow, which is quite different from that of his planning practice. His financial planning work is based on the service he provides, which varies at key times of the year.

This afternoon Mike has an appointment with one of his more interesting clients, a man who writes books and invents things for a living. He always tells Mike about his latest invention or the next one he has planned. The subject of this visit is a review of his portfolio to generate more income. The client explains to Mike that inventions are interesting to develop, but slow to pay off financially. As he listens to his client, Mike realizes how lucky he and Jill are with their insurance business.

Later that afternoon Mike began to review his client's investments to look for methods to increase the income. He drew up a proposal that involved selling some equities with significant profit positions due to earlier purchases at very low share prices. The proceeds could be invested in a ladder of treasuries, thus being fully employed to generate income. The net effect of his thinking allowed Mike to increase the client's annual income by $8,400 or about $700 per month. Mike overlooked his client's request to maintain these stocks as they were recommended by the client's father. He also forgot his client's remark that he expected to do better than treasury securities.

He committed the recommendation to writing and provided an alternative with an annuity, laughing to himself at how easy the exercise had been. Then he put down his client's file and changed screens on his computer to review the last quarter's commission and renewals from the insurance agency. He expected an increase from the prior quarter and was pleasantly surprised with a 14 percent improvement.

When he met with his client again, Mike soon realized how mistaken he had been with his recommendations. The first words from his client's mouth were: "Did you listen to anything I said last week? Honestly, that recommendation could have been made by someone who knew nothing about me!" The client then proceeded to reestablish his parameters to generate income and then rose to leave.

"Let's get together this Monday to review your thoughts. I'm assuming you won't charge me for the time involved in this mistake," to which Mike quickly agreed.

Mike hated to redo work without compensation, but he knew his mind had not been on his client's best interests. Somehow, he had allowed himself to become seriously preoccupied with his other business, the insurance agency. When he thought further, Mike recalled two other incidents in the current quarter when he made significant mistakes in calculations on behalf of a client, mistakes the clients did not realize. He was able to correct one of the errors, but did not correct the other and never told the client.

Conclusion.

Mike has a financial conflict of interest that resides outside of his financial planning practice. Had Mike's conflict created merely a temporary distraction that did not rise to negatively affecting his judgment, the conflict could be called a competing or distracting interest. Let's consider an outside conflict of interest based on an entirely different type of influence, a personal interest.

Personal Conflicts Of Interest

A personal outside of practice conflict of interest is an interest outside of financial planning practice that a financial planner has in another individual (Bearden, 2001). Personal outside conflicts of interest can be interests shared with a client or separate from any client. For example, if a financial planner had a seriously ill friend or relative, that relationship could sufficiently conflict with the planner's judgment to be considered a personal conflict of interest. The professional judgment being impaired would not be the financial planner's judgment on behalf of the person who was the source of the conflict. The financial planner's judgment could be impaired *in general*, with *any* client, if the influence from the outside personal source was sufficiently strong.

If an outside personal conflict of interest lies in an individual who is the financial planner's client, then both the personal interest and the professional interest are focused in the *same* individual. That is the arrangement we will use for an example of an outside of practice personal conflict of interest.

An example.

John Ochua is a fee-only financial planner in New Mexico. Today he is reviewing the file of one of his favorite clients, his little sister Celse. Celse is an attorney and new partner for a small but well-known firm in Roswell. She is single and has an active interest in accumulating funds for retirement and a down payment for a house. As John reviews Celse's file, he notices with satisfaction that she already has saved over six months of income, one of his first recommendations in their first meeting. Their next meeting is this Thursday at nine am.

When the meeting begins, Celse hands an envelope to John. She has a satisfied smile on her face and he wonders what the envelope contains. Upon opening it, John sees a check made out to his sister from her law firm for fifteen thousand dollars. He turns to Celse and asks: "What is this?"

Celse chimes in, as if on cue, "That's my share of the partnership earnings for the six months I was a partner this year! And . . . that's the rest of my house down payment!"

John could tell his sister was very pleased with herself, and he was indeed pleased himself. She was smart and had worked very hard in her first job out of law school. But he felt a welling up of caution as he thought of his youngest sister with no one to depend on but herself.

"Why don't you hold off on the house until the partnership payment next year, Celse? The fifteen thousand will make a nice addition to the savings you've accumulated and you'll be more financially stable then."

Celse could not believe her ears. "Why should I put this in the savings account? I already have ten months of income saved. Now I have enough money to make a 20 percent down payment on the house I want. I don't understand you. I have done everything you have suggested these past five years, and now you're changing your mind."

"You know Celse, I'm just concerned for you. You do not have anyone to rely on but yourself and I want things to go well for you."

"Well, maybe some of the problem is you think I'm still the little sister you had when I was growing up. The youngest in the family by ten years. In case you haven't noticed, I have overcome a number of problems in my adult life. Most of the family really didn't think I would graduate from college, to say nothing of law school. When I passed the bar exam you asked me where I would get a job in Roswell. Well, I know what I can do with my career and I am buying the house. I'm sorry you have less faith in me than my partners do." At that point, Celse slowly rose and left the meeting.

Conclusion.

John has a personal conflict of interest. He has an active interest in his relationship with his sister, which most persons would commend. He also has a client interest in her. As this meeting reflects, the personal interest is stronger than the client interest and generates conflict when the two interests do not agree. More importantly, the personal interest strongly *interferes* with John's objective judgment about his sister's financial plan. He can't stick to his initial recommendations for her because of protective concerns for his sister that extend far beyond his financial planning judgment.

Organizational Conflict of Interest

Some outside conflicts of interest do not involve financial gain or loss and do not involve strong interest in another person. The influence can come from a strong interest in an outside organization. A conflict from interest in an outside organization can have at least three forms. The organization can be one in which the financial planner has a client relationship or one in which the planner has active involvement and/or interest, but has no client relationship. Let's examine two examples, one with a client organization and one in which no client relationship is present.

Example 1.

Marshall Tucker is a financial planner in Des Moines, Iowa. Most of his practice involves personal financial planning, but he does financial planning for several professional organizations.

Marshall is on the Board of Directors for Community Counseling Clinic, a facility that offers counseling for a number of personal and social issues, including marriage counseling, family therapy, counseling for troubled youth and depression therapy. The staff includes licensed counseling psychologists, psychiatric social workers, a psychiatrist, and two ministers certified in clinical pastoral education. Marshall serves as the head of the Finance Committee.

In the January Board meeting, the Clinic received a large donation from a regional foundation. The gift carried the stipulation that the funds were to be used solely for families with troubled youth and carried specific requirements for services that could be funded. When Marshall heard the news of this large influx of funds, he saw an immediate opportunity. For the past two years, he tried to convince the Board that the Clinic should have a comprehensive financial plan. The Board agreed in principal but voted for a limited plan each year, employing Marshall's firm for the work. Marshall suspected the issue was willingness to pay his fee for the comprehensive plan, although the attorney for the Board alluded to not seeing the need for some of the services of a comprehensive plan. Now, in Marshall's mind, funding would not be an issue.

At the next quarterly Board meeting, the head of the professional services committee, Dr. Norley, gave a report of initial allocations of the funding for existing clients, with a preliminary summary of possible future services involving additional staff. The allocations for services to existing clients required approximately one third of the funds provided. Dr. Norley reiterated that the funds had to be used for expenses directly involved in providing services to families with troubled youth.

Marshall thought the doctor's comments were just a smokescreen and the Clinic had much more liberty with the money. "Besides," he reasoned, "the financial health of the clinic is directly involved with the provision of services." This line of thought underscored the merit of a comprehensive financial plan, in Marshall's view. Marshall's fee for the comprehensive plan was $20,000. He called the Chairperson for the Board and reserved time on the agenda of the next meeting to present the case for the plan.

At the next Board meeting, Marshall provided a very professional presentation of the case for a comprehensive financial plan. At the conclusion, the attorney for the Board nodded her head in approval, but suggested that in the best interests of the Clinic, the Board should seek competitive proposals. Marshall initially agreed, but then countered with a key advantage he had over any competing financial planning firm.

"I have served on the Board of the Community Counseling Clinic for three years. In that time, I have provided a limited financial plan and an update for each of the past two years. No other financial planner knows this organization like I do or has the commitment to this organization. Both of those factors will accrue to the benefit of the Clinic and its patients."

The attorney agreed with Marshall's points, but advised that the Board's fiduciary responsibility to the Clinic would be better exercised with competitive presentations. In addition, the attorney alluded to a possible benefit of having an individual less involved with the Clinic consider the work. A second Board member referenced that the present was a slow period for cash flow that would continue through much of the current quarter. The Board accountant agreed and the Board voted to make inquiries to other financial planning firms.

For much of that afternoon and early evening Marshall considered resigning his position on the Board. Board members were not compensated and he spent five to ten hours a month on Clinic business. The financial planning he had done for the Clinic did not cover his expenses. He purposefully charged lower fees, in anticipation of receiving a return later. Now that time seemed remote. If the Clinic began employing an outside firm, his financial planning for the Clinic could be finished. This was the nightmare he initially considered before agreeing to join the Board.

Conclusion for Example 1.

Marshall has a conflict of interest between his desire to develop the Community Counseling Clinic as a client and his fiduciary responsibility to the Clinic as a Board member. He is *compromising* his judgment as a fiduciary of the Clinic to satisfy his interest in developing the Clinic as a financial planning client. In the course of this compromise, Marshall has *also* compromised his judgment as a financial planner, in failure to recognize what is in his *client's best interest*. The Clinic would be better served by interviewing additional planning firms to make an informed decision.

Example 2.

Financial planners also develop conflicts of interest with organizations in which no client relationship is present. Often these interests reflect strong personal interests the planner may have in the mission of the organization. Consider a fictional example. Mary Phelps is a financial planner in Detroit. She is also a Board member and active volunteer with the Downtown Women's Shelter. The Women's Shelter provides temporary living accommodations for women and their children who have suffered physical abuse. Mary has a strong identification with the Shelter from her own history with an abusive ex-husband. In addition to a quarterly Board meeting, she volunteers one night a week providing intake services when new tenants arrive.

Wednesday evening Mary begins her volunteer night at the front desk promptly at 6 pm. This evening would prove to be a demanding one, with seven women, five with children, coming into the shelter. Sometimes when she listened to the women's stories, she flashed back to her unpleasant time with her ex-husband. She always became immobilized with tension for about ten minutes before remembering that her ex-husband was now out of her life. Mary seldom slept well after her volunteer night and this evening would prove to be no different.

The next morning in her office, Mary picked a folder from her client files to review the quarterly portfolio results. During the last quarter, she noted a mutual fund within this client's investments that was under the benchmark mid-point and she made a note to further research the fund in the next quarter. As a beginning point, she checked the research from two independent sources on the fund. Each source indicated the fund would be likely to trend slightly below midpoint for the Lipper classification near term, but could rise above the midpoint for peer funds early the following year.

Mary began to record these observations with a note to maintain the holding, but carefully review the fund and research alternatives in the next quarter. Then she began to think about the last woman with children to enter the Shelter last night. She had been beaten by a boyfriend and was hysterical. Her oldest child, a boy about 9, had a blank gaze on his face and seemed to be in another place.

"How does a child this age witness his mother taking such abuse?" she wondered. Ten minutes went by and she closed and replaced the client folder. She *did not* record her conclusion to keep the fund, her reasons or her decision to review alternatives in the next quarter. She decided the client's investments could last another quarter without the strenuous review she had planned for the current quarter. Without much reflection, Mary realized she had made this decision *several times* in the past with other clients when she had a disturbing night at the Shelter.

Conclusion for Example 2.

Mary has a conflict of interest outside of her financial planning practice that is *directly interfering* with her judgment as a professional. She has such a strong interest in the Shelter where she volunteers that she frequently has difficulty developing the *energy* to use *good professional judgment* in the management of client assets and their financial plans. She probably should find another place to volunteer, one that does not bring up such strong memories and emotional content.

Summary

In this chapter, we considered the conflicts of interest originating outside of financial planning practice. These outside interests rise to the level of impairing the financial planner's professional judgment and thus service to a client. In Chapter 8, we will review the less discussed conflicts of interest that actually develop within practice.

Frank C. Bearden, PhD.

What Registered? An Assessment of Chapter 7

Now you are given the opportunity to test your distinguishing abilities through the concepts and applications of Chapter 7. Please read through the following questions from the chapter, asking if they are true or not and why?

Question # 1 – T or F

For an outside interest to be considered a conflict of interest, the outside interest must damage the financial planner's professional judgment when the planner is in service to the client.

Question # 2 - T or F

An outside financial interest that becomes a conflict of interest for a financial planner is unethical in itself, before considering the influence the interest has on the financial planner's professional judgment.

Question # 3 - T or F

Mike's insurance agency is not a conflict of interest with his financial planning service to his inventor client because Mike agreed to redo his recommendations for his client at no charge.

Question # 4 - T or F

If a financial planner provides financial planning service to a friend and the friendship does not strongly conflict with the professional judgment exercised by the financial planner, the friendship is not a conflict of interest.

Question # 5 - T or F

Mary Phelps' strong commitment to Downtown Women's Shelter can be seen by some as admirable and certainly ethical, so it is exempt from being considered a conflict of interest with her financial planning practice.

The Answers and Why

Question # 1 – T or F

For an outside interest to be considered a conflict of interest, the outside interest must damage the financial planner's professional judgment when the planner is in service to the client.

True. Otherwise the outside interest would not satisfy the key criteria of a conflict of interest, which is damaging professional judgment in service to a client.

Question # 2 - T or F

An outside financial interest that becomes a conflict of interest for a financial planner is unethical in itself, before considering the influence the interest has on the financial planner's professional judgment.

False. An outside financial Interest can be ethical in its own right. The interest produces an unethical outcome when the issue exerts sufficient influence on the financial planner to impair the planner's professional judgment.

Question # 3 - T or F

Mike and his wife's insurance agency is not a conflict of interest with his financial planning service to his inventor client because Mike agreed to redo his recommendations for his client at no charge.

False. The standard for a conflict of interest is impairment of professional judgment. This occurred when the insurance agency generated sufficient influence on Mike that he exercised poor professional judgment in making his initial recommendation, completely forgetting his client's request not to sell the stocks recommended by the client's father.

Question # 4 - T or F

If a financial planner provides financial planning service to a friend and the friendship does not strongly conflict with the professional judgment exercised by the financial planner, the friendship is not a conflict of interest.

True. So long as the outside relationship does not influence the financial planner to use poor professional judgment, the relationship is not a conflict of interest.

Question # 5 - T or F

Mary Phelps' strong commitment to Downtown Women's Shelter can be seen by some as admirable and certainly ethical, so it is exempt from being considered a conflict of interest with her financial planning practice.

False. While Mary's commitment may be admirable and ethical, when it influences her to use poor professional judgment with her financial planning clients, the commitment is a conflict of interest with her professional responsibilities.

CONFLICTS OF INTERESTS WITHIN PRACTICE

CHAPTER 8

In the last chapter we described the more commonly recognized conflicts of interest in financial planning, those in outside of practice. Now we will consider conflicts of interest that are found *within* a practice. Conflicts of interest within a financial planning practice pose the same challenges as conflicts of interest outside of practice, but in a different form. The sources of these conflicts are found in two areas: in the *roles* a financial planner performs when providing service to a client and in the *client relationships* a planner has in the practice (Stark, 2001). The client relationships a financial planner has involve providing service in each role the planner provides for each client.

We should note at this point that the conflicts that arise due to the roles a financial planner plays with a client or the multiple client relationships the planner has rise to being conflicts of interest *only if* the conflicts impair the planner's professional judgment (Bearden, 2009). Short of this standard they are manageable conflicts such as discussed in Chapter 5 and not the primary subject of this book or this chapter

We will examine conflicts of interest within professional roles first. To understand how a conflict of interest can develop within the roles of a financial planning practice, we should first consider the primary roles that professionals play as they serve their principals (known as clients, patients, students or by other names).

Conflicts of Interest among Primary Professional Roles

Professionals can be divided into two groups based on their primary roles of service. Some professionals, such as university teachers, judges, attorneys and journalists emphasize the roles of *critical assessor* and *advocate.* This means that a university professor has an obligation to students to provide both good *critical assessment* of a student's work while also being an *advocate* for the student in the learning process and later professional life (Stark, 2001).

Other professions, such as physicians, engineers, accountants and financial planners emphasize the roles of *diagnostician* and *prescriber of remedies* (Stark, 2001). A financial planner performs the diagnostic role when gathering client financial data and diagnosing financial problems in light of client objectives. The financial planner performs the role of prescribing remedies when making recommendations to the client to resolve or contribute to the resolution of a problem. A financial planner also prescribes remedies if the planner performs implementation services to carry out recommendations.

Before going further, we should note that each profession has all of the roles described above. So, for example, financial planners certainly also provide *critical assessment* when diagnosing a client's financial situation. Financial planners are also *advocates* for their clients. Nonetheless, a profession will utilize one of the two sets of roles as the *primary* modes of service.

How a Primary Role Can Become a Conflict of Interest

The roles of diagnosing a client's financial situation and recommending solutions are vital functions of the financial planning process, and certainly not conflicts of interest in and of themselves. Either of these roles *develops* into a conflict of interest when they are *corrupted* through the exercise of poor professional judgment by the financial planner. Corruption means the roles of diagnosing and recommending solutions take on *more importance* in terms of *time* and *emphasis* than is appropriate. Each role becomes *self-serving* to the *financial planner* rather than to the *client*. Each role becomes an *end in itself*, rather than an important, but limited part in the process of providing financial planning service. In a sense, we can say that poor professional judgment can cause the diagnosing and recommending roles to become *exaggerated* and *distinct* from their proper functions. They take on a different *identity*, becoming corrupted functions rather than appropriate means of professional service.

A simple way to determine if either role has become a conflict of interest is to consider if the *exercise* of the role in service to a client reflects *poor professional judgment.* In addition, the exercise of one exaggerated role that has become a conflict of interest can encourage the financial planner to use poor professional judgment in the other primary role. The diagnostic role, for example, may become a conflict of interest, damaging professional judgment in the diagnosing function, and encouraging poor judgment in the recommending solutions function. To gain clarity in how one of the primary roles in financial planning can become a conflict of interest for the financial planner, let's consider a hypothetical example of this development with each role.

A Conflict of Interest in the Diagnostic Role

A conflict of interest in the diagnostic role becomes a conflict of interest when the financial planner routinely exercises poor professional judgment when carrying out the diagnosing function. This transition can occur if the financial planner is habitually *over impressed* with the severity of client problems and does not form a *clear* summary diagnosis. This poor professional judgment can then render the client unable to understand the planner's analysis. Here is an illustration of how a conflict of interest in the diagnostic role can develop.

An example.

Rolly Burdick is a financial planner in New York City. He does ongoing diagnosis and remedy work with professionals. His remedy role consists of recommendations and implementation work with no or low load financial products. The implementation function he calls "product procurement" and he charges a fee for this service.

In the last few years, Rolly has noticed that his evaluations, even the yearly evaluations of his simpler client situations, have come to take much longer than in his early years of practice. Rolly's explanation for this development has been straightforward: He has more professional knowledge now than in his early years of practice, so he naturally does more research for his clients. Also, he reasons, his clients are growing in their personal and professional lives, so their situations are more complex. The combination of the two, in Rolly's mind, provided a logical understanding of the increased time extended, except for two points. Rolly's clients have begun to complain that his diagnoses are unclear and do not directly lead to his recommendations. Second, Rolly has experienced increasing difficulty developing recommendations that clearly address the problems he diagnoses. He has come to think that many of his clients *just can't be helped.*

Rolly has always been an analytical type, but a difficult situation with a client just a few years ago pushed him into a hyper-analytical mode. In the course of doing retirement planning for a client, Rolly neglected to do an updated asset allocation questionnaire and used a prior allocation to invest a couple's rollover assets. The prior allocation indicated the couples collectively and individually were moderately aggressive investors. Due to their impending retirement, they told Rolly they wanted to be much more conservative with their assets, especially those destined for the IRA rollover account.

Rolly heard the couple, but did not record the comment or perform a new asset allocation. In his diagnosis of the client's investable assets, he failed to note that these assets should be reallocated in light of the couple's change in risk tolerance. His recommendations for the assets involved some minor changes in light of the prior asset allocation. The clients did not catch the mistake and agreed with Rolly's recommendations. He then proceeded to invest the rollover assets, using the prior allocation. Within the next year the market took a significant downturn and the couple lost 35 percent of their retirement assets.

The couple threatened to sue Rolly, but they did not. Nonetheless, he spent the worst six months of his life believing he might be facing financial ruin. He did not want to face this kind of issue again and vowed to be much more thorough in his diagnosis, the source of the prior problem. Now he is usually *unsure* about his diagnostic conclusions, so he doubles his efforts and reviews client issues again. Rolly had become compulsive about his data gathering and diagnosis.

With this development, he found himself losing interest in the recommendations he made. Usually he felt he had omitted a key component in the diagnosis, so the recommendations seemed a little like a waste of time. Rolly has allowed the quality of his judgment with his diagnostic analysis *and* his recommendations to fall from a high level of quality to being just good enough to avoid client complaints. However, recently his clients have begun to notice the deterioration in his work and some have complained to him.

Conclusion.

Rolly's diagnostic role has become a conflict of interest. His exaggeration of the importance of this role of service has led to his providing unclear summary statements to his clients and seemingly incongruent recommendations. His preoccupation with the diagnostic role has damaged his judgment in providing diagnostic analysis *and* financial remedies. He no longer values the remedy role as highly as in the past and his level of service when making recommendations has fallen accordingly.

A Conflict of Interest in the Remedies Role

The role of prescribing remedies can also become so influential to a financial planner that it damages the financial planner's judgment. Conflicts of interest in the remedies role is the most commonly discussed type of conflict of interest within practice, probably because they can involve financial incentive for the financial planner when securing recommended financial products for clients. Cynthia Harrington discussed the prominence of this issue for CPAs who do personal financial planning in the Financial Planning section of *Accounting Today* in an article entitled "Advisor Compensation Tops Conflict of Interest Fears" (2006). The Institute of Chartered Accountants of Australia (ICA) stated in 2006 that financial planners should move to a fee for service model, as the commissions model inherently leads to conflicts of interest (Tuohy). Kenneth Bigel (1998, 2000) has researched financial planners to examine the relationship (if any) between type of compensation (fee, fee-based, or commission only) a financial planner receives and the financial planner's ethical development. Gerald Lins reviewed the potential problems of "soft dollar" compensation for financial planners (1998).

Financial planners engage in the remedies role both in recommending, but not providing financial product remedies and in recommending and providing products. A conflict of interest can develop from the remedies role when a financial planner receives the majority of income from the remedy function through providing financial products. When such a conflict of interest does develop, the instance provides an affirmative answer to Katherine Vessenes' question: "Does my self-interest in this recommendation affect my objectivity" (Vessenes, 1997)? Consider the example of Chelsie, a fee-based financial planner who receives 80 percent of her income from product commissions.

An example.

Chelsie has a general practice involving middle-and upper middle-income clients with various occupations. She began her practice as a totally commission-paid financial planner and later became a Registered Investment Advisor, charging fees for her financial plans. Her initial plans were to use low or no load investment and insurance products for recommendations, charging a fee for her product work. In a client interview a few years ago she received an objection from a client that changed the course of her work. The client resisted her stated fee of $1,000 to assist in securing the products she recommended in the financial plan. The client stated that she understood Chelsie's need to be compensated for this function and would consider competitive products with commissions. Chelsie did a market search and in a few days replaced the initial product recommendations with competitive full-commission products. The client accepted the second group of recommendations and Chelsie's compensation was much higher than her stated fee. From that point forward she began using competitive commission products.

After a year, Chelsie's recommendations from her financial plans began to reflect more new product recommendations. Initially she seldom recommended replacing permanent life insurance policies, but frequently recommended changes in client mutual funds or managed accounts, even when the replacements had only a comparable return history and the former products had some penalty for liquidation. She began to have her recommendations questioned by clients, although no client complained to her or the regulatory authorities. Within the past year Chelsie began reviewing her client's life insurance more closely, frequently recommending replacing existing policies. She got to the point that preparation of a financial plan for new clients or annual reviews for existing clients began with a search for replaceable investment or insurance products. She still performed her diagnostic role, but now her diagnosis was tilted to support any products that could be replaced.

Chelsie's income increased from the life insurance recommendations. She was content that she made a good decision doing the replacements until she received a registered letter from a law firm she did not recognize. One of her clients was suing her for recommending a change in life insurance from a policy with a standard rating to a new policy with a higher rating for health issues. The client received a refund of premiums from the policy recommended by Chelsie and was able to reinstate the prior policy, after which the lawsuit was dropped. Chelsie was required to respond to an inquiry by the insurance department of her state, which was accepted with no further action.

Conclusion.

Chelsie's remedies role has grown in influence until it became a conflict of interest. Cordell and Lemoine (2009) addressed issues a financial planner should consider to maintain fiduciary responsibility (and not become the means for a conflict of interest) when recommending life insurance products to a client. Now her diagnostic role has also become corrupted and a conflict of interest, centered primarily on supporting the replacement of products.

Some financial planners will sincerely state that any planner who receives commissions for product placement has an inherent conflict of interest. Other financial planners will counter that no conflict is present if the financial planner receiving the commissions provides thorough disclosure of all the ways the planner is compensated. The thesis of this book is that there is a third, more useful standard to determine a conflict of interest based on the resulting quality of the professional judgment of the financial planner. Following this thought, Chelsie does not have a conflict of interest because she receives commissions for product placement, but because her professional judgment has been Impaired to the point of recommending objectively inferior or inappropriate products just so she will receive commissions.

A key point to remember when reviewing these hypothetical examples is the diagnosing and prescribing roles have a proper emphasis or balance in financial planning practice. Conflicts of interest begin to grow in either role when the role becomes *exaggerated* beyond its rightful place in practice due to the exercise of poor professional judgment. Now let's consider conflicts of interest that can develop among client relationships.

Conflicts of Interest with Client Relationships

A conflict of interest can develop when one or more client relationships becomes *corrupted*, so that the financial planner's judgment is impaired. For example, a financial planner's relationship with a client who represents a large share of the revenue of a practice can become of sufficient concern that the planner begins to use poor judgment with the client. If the pattern of poor judgment continues and becomes habitual with the client, the client relationship has become *corrupted* and a conflict of interest. The corrupted client relationship also can lead to bad professional judgment in work with other clients. This may be as simple as a poor allocation of time among clients. Consider this example to see how such a situation can develop.

An example.

James is a fee-only financial planner in Seattle. His works almost exclusively with physicians, beginning with an acquaintance he met several years earlier at the medical school. This acquaintance became a client and promotes James' practice to newly graduating medical students. James' most affluent client is also his most profitable, a middle aged heart surgeon with a well-established practice. Last year the surgeon provided almost 10 percent of the revenue to the practice.

In a recent meeting with the client, the heart surgeon client explained that he was going to expand his practice, buying the practice of a retiring surgeon and hiring another heart surgeon who just completed her residency. The client told James the practice would double its revenue in three years. Within this in mind, he made an appointment with James to discuss the expansion and make some changes in his financial plan. In the meeting, he told James their business was going to significantly increase and he would need much more of James' time. James decided then that he would do whatever was needed to increase his work with the client.

Allocating the time needed quickly turned to spending *excessive* time with the heart surgeon's financial matters. In addition, James developed a hesitancy to speak candidly when he and his client met. He developed an apprehension that the client might leave his firm if James provided a contrary opinion to some of the doctor's ideas. His mode of operating with this client became reduced to recommending small changes in the financial plan and accommodating any of the client's suggestions. James had suspended his *best professional judgment* in the name of pleasing and keeping his most profitable client. The client became a conflict of interest for whom James no longer exercised his best professional judgment.

In addition, the bad judgment James now chronically used with the heart surgeon began to influence his judgment with *other* clients. Initially James planned to hire another paraplanner part-time to handle some of the increased work the heart surgeon client provided. Upon reflection, he held off on the new staff member, reasoning that he could handle most of the additional work without more staff. He reviewed the services he and the existing paraplanner provided for other clients and eliminated some significant areas of review that he now thought of less importance.

James' other clients slowly felt the impact of his increasing involvement with the heart surgeon and his employees. Phone calls were returned in two days, rather than the next day, which had been the norm. Mistakes began to show up in the input data and calculations of financial plans. Finally, a client called James to complain that someone in the financial planning office had forged the client's signature on an important document. Two clients sent letters stating a severing of relationship with the firm. James did not take these occurrences as signs of a larger problem. Instead, he told himself that he and his staff were handling the client service adequately. He was anxious to view the first quarter results for the practice, to see how the increased business showed up in revenue and expenses. He reasoned that after two quarters he would be able to see a significant increase in net income to the firm.

Conclusion.

James' relationship with the largest client in the office had become a conflict of interest, distorting his judgment about service to the client and to James' remaining clients. Rather than exercising sound professional judgment, disagreeing with his most profitable client when appropriate, and hiring the part-time paraplanner now that he had the business to support the expense, James came to focus on the increased profitability he believed his firm was sure to realize. He minimized the importance of continued quality service to his other clients and chose to reduce their service. He planned no reduction in his fees to match the reduction in service.

We should note, however, that the experience of James exercising bad judgment by providing poor service to other clients is quite different from a financial planner deciding that some clients are not sufficiently profitable to merit the financial planner's further service. The first is the use of bad judgment under the influence of a conflict of interest (a corrupt client relationship), while the second can be an exercise of sound professional judgment in light of the facts in a practice.

Summary

In this chapter, we discussed the conflicts of interest that develop within a financial planning practice. This closes our discussion of the origins of conflicts of interest for financial planners. In a later chapter we will review remedies for conflicts of interest. In Chapter 9 we will address the two primary ways a financial planner can determine if a conflict of interest is present. Emphasis will be placed on the method that does the least harm to the client.

What Registered? An Assessment of Chapter 8

Now you have the opportunity to test your distinguishing abilities through the concepts and applications of Chapter 8. . Please read through the following questions from the chapter, asking if they are true or not and why?

Question # 1 - T or F

Conflicts of interest within a financial planning practice are the natural conflicts that develop between the roles a financial planner plays in serving clients, the various client relationships the planner has, and the planner's professional interest in his or her clients.

Question # 2 - T or F

Rolly Burdick became hyper-analytical in his diagnostic role of service due to a mistake he made and a resulting threat of a lawsuit by clients. As a result, his diagnostic role became a conflict of interest against his professional interest in his clients, damaging his professional judgment.

Question # 3 - T or F

Chelsie's recommendation of commissioned life insurance policies as part of her financial plan was inherently a conflict of interest, as she stood to benefit from the compensation of products her financial plan recommended.

Question # 4 - T or F

James' relationship with his most profitable client, a heart surgeon, is a conflict of interest because this client is James' largest source of income.

Question # 5 - T or F

A key point to remember about conflicts of interest that originate with practice is they develop from corruption of what are otherwise constructive roles of service or client relationships.

The Answers and Why

Question # 1 - T or F

Conflicts of interest within a financial planning practice are the natural conflicts that develop between the roles a financial planner plays in serving clients, the various client relationships the planner has, and the planner's professional interest in his or her clients.

False. The roles a financial planner plays in service and client relationships do not provide sufficient conflict with the financial planner's professional interest in clients to impair the planner's professional judgment, the key indicator of a conflict of interest. Roles of service and client relationships can *become* conflicts of interest when they become corrupted, taking on more importance than is appropriate. Roles of service and client relationships then become self-serving to the financial planner rather than the client.

Question # 2 - T or F

Rolly Burdick became hyper-analytical in his diagnostic role of service due to a mistake he made and a resulting threat of a lawsuit by clients. As a result, his diagnostic role became a conflict of interest against his professional interest in his clients, damaging his professional judgment.

True. Rolly's anxiety over the prospect of being sued due to a past mistake did not subside and he became chronically *unsure* about his diagnostic conclusions. As a consequence, he doubled his efforts, becoming compulsive about his data gathering and diagnosis, against his better professional judgment.

Question # 3 - T or F

Chelsie's recommendation of commissioned life insurance policies as part of her financial plan was inherently a conflict of interest, as she stood to benefit from the compensation of products her financial plan recommended.

False. The recommendation of financial products that generate additional compensation to the financial planner is a conflict of interest only if the recommendation damages the financial planner's professional judgment. Chelsie allowed her recommendations role to grow to inappropriate proportions, becoming corrupted, so that she began preparation of each financial plan with a search for replaceable investment or insurance products. Even her work in diagnosing client financial problems became tilted solely to support any products that could be replaced. In this corrupt form, her recommendations role became a conflict of interest against her professional judgment.

Question # 4 - T or F

James' relationship with his most profitable client, a heart surgeon, is a conflict of interest because this client is James' largest source of income.

False. A client's contribution to a financial planner's income is not a conflict of interest unless this fact impairs the financial planner's professional judgment. In James' case, his relationship with the client came to take on more importance than appropriate, becoming corrupted. His method of operation with this client was reduced to recommending small changes in the financial plan, while agreeing with all of the client's suggestions. James suspended his best professional judgment to please his most profitable client. The client relationship did not begin as a conflict of interest, but subsequently became one as the relationship was corrupted.

Question # 5 - T or F

A key point to remember about conflicts of interest that originate with practice is they develop from corruption of what are otherwise constructive roles of service or client relationships.

True. The roles of service a financial planner provides and the client relationships he or she enjoys are not conflicts of interest until they are given inappropriate significance, becoming corrupted from their constructive functions within financial planning practice.

INDICATIONS OF THEIR PRESENCE

CHAPTER 9

How does a financial planner recognize a conflict of interest in practice? Said differently, once a financial planner has some understanding of conflicts of interest, how can the planner recognize the symptoms that indicate their presence? Conflicts of interest can be recognized in two ways, beginning with the symptom of *poor work product* or beginning with the symptom of *poor professional judgment*, using the judgment test.

Beginning with Poor Work Product

As we have discussed in earlier chapters, conflicts of interest will damage professional judgment if not addressed. They also will produce damaged work product in the form of bad advice, given verbally or in written form through a financial plan. Many conflicts of interest are recognized after the fact by looking back from poor work product to poor professional judgment, and then to the conflict that produced the lapse in judgment. We should remember that all poor work product is not explained by a conflict of interest, as many other explaining influences are possible. However, conflicts of interest are a viable explanation to consider.

Any of the examples of conflicts of interest that we have used to this point can illustrate how the same financial planner could have realized the source of his or her problem by starting with poor work product and working back to poor professional judgment. The most recent example involved James, the financial planner who was overly impressed with the influence of his most financially rewarding client. This influence led James to use poor judgment when providing service to this client and his other clients. James could have realized his conflict of interest by looking at the work product he came to provide for this client. Had he taken the time to review his recent recommendations, he would have realized that he had exchanged his best judgment for the decision to make only minor changes and agree with all of the client's suggestions. In addition, James would have seen that he was providing poor quality work for his *other* clients by taking twice the time to return phone calls, supervising and approving inaccurate work with client calculations, and *not* catching a forgery of a client's signature. He had clearly lowered his work standard.

If the financial planner asked himself *why* he lowered his work standards, he would have realized that he first lowered his work standards for his most profitable client, doing so because he because he became overly impressed with the financial benefit this client could bring him. His most profitable client had become a conflict of interest for the financial planner in his work with *this* client and his other clients.

Recognizing a conflict of interest by reviewing bad work product has the benefit of allowing a financial planner to definitely identify the source of the problem. However, reviewing work product and admitting quality of work slippage is a tough thing to do. In a practice with only one financial planner, the planner could consider reviewing his work product on a regular basis, at least annually, to ask if the overall work product, including financial plan, recommendations, implementation if any, meets the standard of good professional judgment. In a practice with more than one financial planner, the preferable way of doing this would involve having another planner review the work. Using regularly scheduled work product reviews does provide a method to detect poor work product, albeit after the impact of poor professional judgment has been delivered.

This brings us to the key drawback of using work product as a method to discover a conflict of interest. The method brings a significant drawback to the client. Bad work product means the client must experience the *results* of the financial planner's poor judgment *before* the source of the poor judgment can be found. So the client has to lose first. That result makes the poor work product method useful after the fact, but not desirable before the fact.

Beginning with a Test of Judgment

Beginning with a test of judgment to determine a conflict of interest enables a financial planner to make a determination *before* exercising poor professional judgment and creating faulty work product at the client's expense. The test begins with the financial planner asking if professional judgment will be impaired by an influence that is conflicting with the planner's professional interest in a client. Will the tide of the influence rise high enough to topple the balance of the financial planner's good judgment?

The test of judgment brings a big advantage to client, for the client has the active possibility of avoiding the financial planner's bad judgment and resulting work product. This advantage will be realized if the financial planner is able to recognize the bad judgment that will result from the interest producing the conflict. However, the test of judgment is often a difficult test for a financial planner to complete. We discussed earlier in this book that a conflict of interest exerts a powerful influence on a professional. For this reason, as Davis has pointed out, a professional can easily overlook a conflict of interest or misjudge how much it will affect the professional's judgment (Davis, 2001). The net effect is the financial planner may believe he or she is exercising good judgment for the client, when in fact the financial planner may be *compromising* the well-being of the client for the benefit of the interest causing the conflict. As an example, the financial planner with the successful real estate broker client in Chapter 2 may have initially thought entering a business relationship with his client would help their financial planning relationship. So how can a financial planner *accurately* exercise a test of judgment?

Triangulation.

Since a conflict of interest can pose a serious problem for a financial planning practice, more than one viewpoint should be gathered about the conflict. I suggest using a technique that researchers call *triangulation.* Bruce Berg, a renowned scholar in qualitative research methodology, described the technique this way: "By combining several lines of sight, researchers obtain a better, more substantive picture of reality. . . The use of multiple lines of sight is frequently called *triangulation*" (Berg, 1998, p. 4-5). Another recognized scholar in the field of qualitative research, John Creswell, stated triangulation "involves corroborating evidence from difference sources to shed light on a theme or perspective" (1998, p. 202).

Using triangulation in a financial planning practice would involve gathering three lines of sight on a potential conflict of interest. The first line of sight is the financial planner's own assessment of the conflict. The second view should be the judgment from a trusted and respected professional peer. The financial planner providing the second opinion should have no involvement with the conflicting interest, the client or the practice of the conflicted planner. The client and the conflicting influence should be presented without identifying information.

The third source of the triangulation should come from the judgment of a trusted adjacent professional like a CPA, attorney or trust officer. These professionals also take on fiduciary responsibility with clients and understand the importance of providing sound professional judgment and work product. The adjacent professional, like the peer financial planner, should have no involvement with the interest generating the conflict, the client or the practice of the conflicted planner.

From these three sources, a financial planner will have sufficient information to decide if the conflicting interest will impair his or her professional judgment. If the financial planner believes his or her professional judgment is at risk after reviewing the situation and consulting with these two professional sources, the planner can assume a conflict of interest probably *is* involved and can decide upon an appropriate remedy. (Triangulation can also be useful if a financial planner uses the review of prior work product method discussed earlier to determine if quality if work has slipped and if a conflict of interest is the cause.)

Radar to Catch the Symptoms

To this point we have discussed two methods of recognizing a conflict of interest in a financial planning practice. We have demonstrated that the test of judgment using three sources of evaluation (triangulation) is the best choice because it allows the financial planner to act on early symptoms of a conflict of interest and avoid the cost of poor judgment and work product for the client. Now we should ask where a financial planner should look for initial symptoms of a conflict of interest. Where is the *radar* the planner can use to catch the initial *blip* or *symptom* of a conflict of interest?

The planner's *own awareness* is an important first indicator if symptoms are present. Does *the planner* feel conflicted by an issue to the point of having professional judgment affected? In psychological terms this is known as cognitive dissonance, and means the discomfort arising from holding two conflicting thoughts at the same time (Festinger, 1957). But as with the test of professional judgment, one line of sight is not enough. A financial planner should have additional sources to provide adequate *indications* of possible conflicts of interest in development.

Two additional sources are available in most financial planning practices. The first is easy to miss because the source is so obvious--clients. Because a client has a different viewpoint than the financial planner, the client may recognize signs of a conflict of interest that the financial planner does not notice. A client on occasion may sense that the financial planner is conflicted in work done for the client or another client. When a client voices concern about a possible conflict, the issue should be taken seriously and appropriately addressed. A client should be viewed as another set of eyes and ears that has the most to gain or lose in the quality of a financial planner's professional judgment and work product.

In addition, the financial planner's staff, including administrative, paraprofessional, and professional associates, can be an additional source of indications of a possible conflict of interest. The principal (s) in the planning firm should provide an orientation to conflicts of interest for all staff, with examples, so the awareness level of personnel is good. In addition, the principal (s) should encourage feedback from staff when a staff member feels a comment is appropriate.

An early indication of a conflict of interest can be deterioration in a financial planner's behavior before the planner begins to feel any sense of conflict from the conflicting issue. The financial planner could begin to display poor judgment on behalf of a client due to the influence of the conflict of interest, without initial awareness of the source or nature of his or her behavior. In these instances, a peer associate may spot the problem before serious damage is done to the client. Professional peers in the same practice can provide this service, as only symptoms (and not a determination) of a conflict of interest are being sought. For this type of communication between a peer financial planner and the conflicted planner to be effective requires a strong trusting relationship between the two, as well as high self-esteem by the financial planner with the conflict.

Feedback from clients and staff members may indicate the appearance of a conflict of interest rather than an actual conflict. In these instances, the main point of Chapter 6 applies: the perceptions of key individuals in the practice should be taken seriously and addressed, even if proven factually incorrect upon closer examination. A financial planner will have a much better opportunity to keep conflicts of interest from developing in the practice by taking an inclusive view of all symptoms of possible conflicts of interest, his or her own perceptions and those of clients and staff.

Summary

In this chapter we reviewed the two methods a financial planner can use to determine if a conflict of interest is present in work with a client. We stated that a financial planner can work backward from bad work product, through poor professional judgment, to a conflict of interest when a strong conflict is the source of the poor judgment. A financial planner can also begin with the awareness of the conflict and assess the likelihood of resulting poor judgment and work product. This method can save the client from the experience of bad work product.

We then moved to the recognition that while the financial planner is the primary *instrument* for recognizing conflicts of interest, the planner should use other sources to insure that recognition of these conflicts is as quick and sure as possible. Clients and profession staff can provide these additional sources. In Chapter 9 we will discuss appropriate remedies when a financial planner recognizes a conflict of interest.

What Registered? An Assessment of Chapter 9

You now have the opportunity to test your distinguishing abilities through the concepts and applications of Chapter 9. Please read through the following questions

Question # 1 - T or F

The key drawback to using poor work product as a method to recognize a conflict of interest is the inaccuracy of the method.

Question # 2 – T or F

Triangulation is a method that a financial planner can use to accurately determine if a conflict will impair the planner's professional judgment. The method involves exposing the conflict to three lines of sight from three persons.

Question # 3 – T or F

A financial planner's own awareness is an important first source of information that a conflict of interest is present, even if planner does not sense the symptoms of the conflict.

Question # 4 – T or F

Because a client has a different point of view than the financial planner, the client may recognize indications of a conflict of interest that the financial planner does not notice.

Question # 5 – T or F

The perceptions of key persons within a practice regarding a conflict of interest should be taken seriously only to respect the viewpoints of these individuals.

The Answers and Why

Question # 1 - T or F

The key drawback to using poor work product as a method to recognize a conflict of interest is the inaccuracy of the method.

False. With candor from the financial planner and the use of triangulation, the poor work product method is an accurate method to determine a conflict of interest. The key drawback of using poor work product as an indicator is a client has to experience the poor work product first before an analysis can be made to determine the reasons for the low quality.

Question # 2 – T or F

Triangulation is a method that a financial planner can use to accurately determine if a conflict will impair the planner's professional judgment. The method involves exposing the conflict to three lines of sight from three persons.

True. Triangulation also can be used to determine the extent and origins of poor work product, often exposing conflicts of interest.

Question # 3 – T or F

A financial planner's own awareness is an important first source of information that a conflict of interest is present, even if planner does not sense the symptoms of the conflict.

False. If the financial planner does not sense that his or her professional judgment will be damaged by another interest, the planner's perceptual radar may not be a good indicator of an impending problem. Triangulation is the best way to be sure.

Question # 4 – T or F

Because a client has a different point of view than the financial planner, the client may recognize indications of a conflict of interest that the financial planner does not notice.

True. A client's vantage point can provide a significant addition to that of the financial planner, capturing a key symptom of compromised professional judgment that the financial planner does not realize.

Question # 5 – T or F

The perceptions of key persons within a practice regarding a conflict of interest should be taken seriously only to respect the viewpoints of these individuals.

False. While this is a good reason to take the viewpoints of key persons in a practice seriously, there is an additional reason. The perceptions of key individuals may be accurate and reflect a conflict of interest.

REMEDIES

CHAPTER 10

When a financial planner recognizes a conflict of interest, what should the planner do? Before reviewing constructive solutions for conflicts of interest, we should consider the founding premise of *any* useful remedy: A financial planner is *most likely* to provide sound professional judgment when *not influenced by* or *exerting the energy to resist* a conflict of interest. The influence, if left unaddressed, *will damage* professional judgment. Resisting a conflict of interest, without *eliminating* the conflict, requires *more effort* than a financial planner can expend and maintain sound judgment. In addition, the effort is fruitless in the long run, for a conflict of interest, if not removed, by definition *will prevail* and result in *damaged judgment*. All conflicts that can be effectively resisted are temporary distractions and not conflicts of interest.

Effective remedies for a conflict of interest are determined by where the conflict of interest originates. Conflicts outside of practice and conflicts inside of practice require different solutions to remove the influence of the conflict of interest from the financial planner's sphere of practice. We will begin the discussion of remedies with the best-known conflicts of interest, those originating outside of practice (Stark, 2001).

Conflicts of Interest Outside of Practice
Removing the Source

The first and best choice of remedies for conflicts of interest outside of practice is to remove the source of the conflict. This allows the financial planner to accept or maintain the client engagement without the risk to professional judgment. How would a financial planner do this? We can view the situation described in Chapter 1 involving Maurice Wills and his commercial realtor client Mark Swinson as a good example.

Maurice Wills is a financial planner who compromised his best professional judgment for an outside business venture with his client. The incident reviewed in Chapter 1 occurred after the outside venture was already established. However, the development of the conflict of interest began when the client first broached the possibility of the outside venture to the financial planner. The influence of the outside business venture *and* the opportunity to avoid the influence started then. If the financial planner had sought to maintain his level of professional judgment in service to his client, he would have politely refused the offer of the venture in the name of upholding the quality of the client relationship. This decision might have presented Wills with an initial awkward moment with his client, but would have been a sound investment in the value of work he sought to provide in his financial planning practice.

Frank C. Bearden, PhD.

Often the conflict of interest has a foothold in the financial planning relationship *before* it is admitted and faced. If Maurice Wills chose to face his conflict of interest now, with the real estate relationship in place, what could he do? If he wanted to continue the financial planning relationship with Mark Swinson, he could consider selling his outside interests to his client. That would remove the source of conflict with the financial planning relationship. If Maurice felt the outside venture was more important than his client relationship with Mark or if selling his interest could not be accomplished at the present time, Wills could consider the second recommended remedy, which we will now discuss.

Refusing or Resigning the Engagement

A financial planner may decide that removing the source of the conflict of interest is not wise. Such a decision is usually based on the financial planner's assessment of the value of the interest. In the case of Maurice Wills, he could well decide that the present and long-term value of his real estate investments was too much to forego. In the case of a *personal* conflict of interest, the financial planner could simply decide that the personal relationship was too important to give up. In the case of the financial planner John Ochua in Chapter 7, the personal relationship is with his sister. While John has made a mistake in professional judgment due to his concern for his sister, he would probably be unwilling to lose his personal relationship with her. So what can the financial planner do? If the planner values the quality of his or her professional judgment, the financial planner can and should consider refusing or resigning the engagement, maintaining the outside interest. We should note here that refusing to provide service to a prospective client in light of a conflicting interest (such as a personal or commercial relationship) with the same person may produce some temporary discomfort in the prospective client and the other interest or relationship.

Disclosure

An important part of the financial planner's responsibility when removing the source of the conflict or refusing or resigning an engagement is to explain the professional reasons for the decision. This process is not as easy as it may sound. The financial planner should emphasize the importance of being able to provide his or her best judgment and insight on behalf of the client, unencumbered by any significant conflicting influence. The financial planner should explain that a conflict of interest, such as the non-planning interest in the client, will impair the planner's judgment in financial planning work done for the client. Hence, the financial planner cannot maintain the outside interest and continue to provide quality service to the client.

If the financial planner decides to maintain the outside interest and refuse or resign the engagement, the financial planner should state that he or she values the outside relationship sufficiently that another financial planner should be sought. With non-personal conflicts, the financial planner risks the possibility that the client may suggest the planning relationship continue and the outside relationship end. If this occurs, the planner will have to decide how to accommodate the client's wishes. If the financial planner decides to refuse or resign the engagement, the planner should assure the client that the planner will recommend more than one respected peer financial planner to continue providing service.

Temporary Remedies When the Conflict Cannot Be Resolved Quickly

Occasionally a financial planner is faced with a situation in which a conflict of interest outside of practice cannot be resolved quickly. Either the source of the conflict cannot be removed in a timely manner (or at all, with a personal conflict) or the engagement cannot be refused or ended quickly. Let's consider two examples. First, if the outside conflict is a personal relationship, such as a close friendship, a romantic relationship, or a relative, the financial planner may decide to maintain the relationship and refer the client to other professional financial planning sources. But what if no other financial planning sources are readily available? Second, if the outside conflict is due to a business relationship, what if the client and financial planner desire to maintain the financial planning relationship, but the business relationship cannot be ended quickly due to market and other timing constraints? What should the financial planner do?

In situations when a conflict of interest cannot be resolved promptly, the financial planner must remember one key point: The effort to resist a conflict of interest must be *temporary* or the conflict itself must be temporary. If the conflict of interest is not temporary, professional judgment eventually *will suffer, as will the client and the financial planner.* With this thought firmly in mind, the financial planner should disclose the conflict of interest to the client. Assuming the client wants to continue the engagement, the financial planner then should exert the extra effort required to resist the influence of the conflict. This will allow the financial planner temporarily to provide sound professional judgment to the client until the planning relationship can be resigned or the source of the conflict of interest can be removed.

In summary, when a financial planner has a new or existing conflict of interest outside of practice, the planner should seek a way to remove the interest that is the source of the conflict or refuse or resign the engagement. Any other measure must be temporary, and is doomed to fail if prolonged.

Let's change topics slightly now and look to conflicts of interest originating within practice. What can a financial planner do when the conflict of interest has developed *within* the financial planning practice?

Conflicts of Interest within the Practice

Conflicts of interest originating in the practice pose the same challenges as those outside of practice, but in different forms. As we referenced in Chapter 8, a conflict of interest in a financial planning practice develops from one of the primary *roles* the financial planner performs for a client or from the *relationships* the financial planner has with clients. Let's recall that the two primary roles of service provided by a financial planner are the *diagnostic* and *remedies* roles.

When either of the professional *roles* a financial planner provides or a *client relationship itself* develops into a conflict of interest, the *role* or *client relationship* becomes *corrupted*, taking on importance beyond the rightful boundaries of its position within the practice. The role of service or client relationship becomes a *different entity* from a *constructive* role or client relationship, a *habitual* example of bad practice that will exert damaging influence on the financial planner's judgment. A corrupted diagnostic or remedies role or a corrupted client relationship is the type of conflict of interest a financial planner may encounter within his or her practice. How should a financial planner effectively deal with these conflicts?

Removing the Source

Conflict from a corrupted diagnostic role. Removing the source of the conflict of interest is always the first recommended remedy because this action will allow the financial planner to accept or continue the engagement. When the diagnostic or remedy role becomes corrupted and exerts sufficient distraction to the financial planner that the financial planner fails to exercise sound professional judgment in carrying out the role, the corrupted role itself becomes the source of the conflict. In this case, removing the source involves *recasting* the role. Recasting means the role first must be redefined in terms of the financial planner's best professional judgment. Among other considerations, the financial planner's judgment would allow the role to be performed with a high level of quality, in a reasonable time frame, with allowance for the financial planner's other responsibilities with the same and other clients. Consulting with peer financial planners is recommended to help the financial planner gain clarity in restoring sound professional judgment to a corrupted professional role.

But redefining the professional role is not sufficient to remove the financial planner's conflict of interest. The financial planner must also apply disciplined *implementation* of the redefined role, to continually support the appropriate perspective for the role. A corrupted professional role is recast only when *both* redefined and implemented. Otherwise, the planner will revert back to former habits and the conflict of interest will remain or return.

Let's consider an example, looking to the situation of Rolly Burdick. He is the financial planner in Chapter 7, whose over-emphasis of his *diagnostic* role with clients became a conflict of interest, impairing his professional judgment in both his diagnosing and remedy roles. To remove the conflict of interest within his practice, Rolly must *recast* his diagnostic role, restoring appropriate limits to the time and effort dedicated to the role. This will eliminate the exaggerated influence of the role, removing potential damage to his professional judgment in providing service as a financial diagnostician as well as a provider of remedies. When recasting is completed and maintained, the diagnostic role will no longer be a conflict of interest. Rolly will experience restored professional judgment in diagnosing problems and making recommendations for clients.

Conflict from a corrupted remedy role. A corrupted remedy role can result in a variety of ways from poor professional judgment. One example in which this can occur is referenced in Chapter 7 with Chelsie, a fee-based financial planner who received a majority of income from providing financial products as part of the remedy service. Timothy Lynch reminds us that this does not inevitably occur, comparing commission compensation with fees received by other professionals such as physicians and attorneys (Lynch, 2009). What should a financial planner do when the planner realizes the remedy role has become corrupted, exerting undue and inappropriate influence on the financial planner's judgment? Removing the source of the conflict through *recasting* is the best solution. With the example of Chelsie, the financial planner must *reshape* her recommending remedies function to *conform* to her best professional judgment, rather than allowing the conflict of interest to *shape* her judgment. In the process of redefining the way she provides remedies, perhaps she might reconsider her original idea of providing no and low load financial products, realizing most of her compensation from fees charged for the service of procuring appropriate products. Redefining her perspective of recommending and providing remedies with sound professional judgment and implementing that redefinition will eliminate the influence of what was once a conflict of interest. As with all in practice conflicts of interest, disciplined implementation will ultimately determine if the conflict is eliminated or remains.

Conflict from a corrupted client relationship. As we discussed in Chapter 8, conflicts of interest within practice can also involve a corrupted client relationship. Corruption can occur with a client who represents a large portion of the financial planner's revenue. The example of James and the heart surgeon client can illustrate how a conflict of interest with a client can be removed through recasting the client relationship to one reflecting sound professional judgment. As this relationship is reformed under the dictates of the financial planner's best professional judgment, the planner should allocate an appropriate amount of time for the client and resume providing his *best* professional opinion to the client, even when he senses disagreement. In other words, James should regain his professional confidence with this client and implement the sound judgment and practice that will follow. As a result of recasting his relationship with the client, James should reconsider his decision not to hire an additional paraplanner as well as the decision to eliminate some of the areas of review work he formerly did for clients. As the recasting is reinforced with sustained practice, the influence of the former conflict of interest will be eliminated as a detrimental factor to James' professional judgment and work product.

What if the Client Does Not Agree?

When a financial planner decides to recast roles of service or a corrupted client relationship to the planner's best financial judgment, the client may not be willing to go along with the new arrangement. The financial planner has a professional obligation to be persuasive about the benefits of the revitalized client relationship. If the client insists on the prior relationship, the financial planner will have to consider the merits of continuing the engagement. The controlling factor for the financial planner in this situation is knowledge that he or she has restored professional judgment to its rightful place in carrying out the financial planner's fiduciary obligation to clients.

Refusing or Resigning the Engagement

Refusing or resigning the engagement is not a constructive *first* course of action for a conflict of interest originating within practice. This is because the decision does not address the real problem, which is a corrupted role of service or a corrupt client relationship. If the financial planner refused or resigned an engagement without first seeking to recast the corrupted role or client relationship, the problem would probably continue with other engagements because the source of the corruption had not been faced and resolved.

As we discussed earlier in this chapter, refusing or resigning an engagement *is* an effective remedy for an outside of practice conflict of interest because the source of the conflict is outside of the practice. Keeping the interest out of the practice by refusing or resigning the engagement *does* resolve the conflict, in that the financial planner's attention then is not conflicted between the outside interest and focus on a client. The financial planner is then able to provide unconflicted focus and professional judgment to other clients who do not bring the same or other strong outside interests into the planner's practice.

Summary

This has been the "What should I do now?" chapter that presents appropriate remedies for conflicts of interest both outside of and within financial planning practice. The remedies are not easy, but they do directly address removing the conflicting interest from the influence of the financial planner's professional judgment. We have discussed how with outside of practice conflicts of interest the interest can be removed or the engagement can be refused or terminated. We have discussed temporary measures that sometimes must be used until the influence of the conflicting interest can be removed from the planner's sphere of influence.

Inside of practice conflicts of interest pose the same challenges as out of practice conflicts, but in a different form. The process of recasting the professional role or relationship(s) must be performed to eliminate the influence of the conflict of interest. Recasting is more than redefining a role or relationship. Recasting has a lasting impact only if the redefinition is implemented and maintained. Chapter 11 provides some suggestions about the practice policy of a financial planning professional regarding conflicts of interest.

What Registered? An Assessment of Chapter 10

Now you have the opportunity to test your distinguishing abilities through the concepts and applications of Chapter 10. Please read through the following questions

Question # 1 - T or F

The remedy for a conflict of interest of removing the source of the conflict assumes a financial planner should not plan long term to resist the conflict and continue to exercise good judgment on behalf of a client.

Question # 2 - T or F

The remedy for a conflict of interest of refusing or resigning the engagement assumes a financial planner does not value an engagement with the prospective or existing client.

Question # 3 - T or F

When a financial planner encounters a conflict of interest within practice, redefining the role of service (diagnostic or remedies) or the client relationship will realign the role of service or client relationship to its rightful place in practice and the planner again will be able to exercise sound professional judgment on behalf of clients.

Question # 4 - T or F

A client will always be agreeable when a financial planner proposes a remedy for the influence of a conflict of interest, because eliminating the influence is to the client's benefit, as the client will not receive poor work product from the financial planner.

The Answers and Why

Question # 1 - T or F

The remedy for a conflict of interest of removing the source of the conflict assumes a financial planner should not plan long term to resist the conflict and continue to exercise sound professional judgment on behalf of a client.

True. Conflicts of interest by definition *will* damage professional judgment. A conflict that does not damage professional judgment is a distraction and not a conflict of interest. Distractions can be overcome so that professional judgment can be maintained. A conflict of interest may be resisted on a temporary basis and professional judgment maintained, but the conflict of interest will prevail at an unexpected time, with negative consequences to the client and the financial planner.

Question # 2 - T or F

The remedy for a conflict of interest of refusing or resigning the engagement assumes a financial planner does not value an engagement with the prospective or existing client.

False. When a financial planner refuses or resigns an engagement due to a conflict of interest, the planner may well value the engagement. However, the financial planner values the outside conflict of interest more than forming or maintaining the engagement, such as the value placed on a close personal relationship or a business venture.

Question # 3 - T or F

When a financial planner encounters a conflict of interest within practice, redefining the role of service (diagnostic or remedies) or the client relationship will realign the role of service or client relationship to its rightful place in practice and the planner again will be able to exercise sound professional judgment on behalf of clients.

False. Redefining the role of service or the client relationship is a good beginning, but is not enough. The role of service or client relationship must be *recast*, which means disciplined follow through must be exercised so the role or relationship is changed in fact. Then the conflict of interest will be removed from the practice and the financial planner will be able to exercise sound professional judgment.

Question # 4 - T or F

A client will always be agreeable when a financial planner proposes a remedy for the influence of a conflict of interest, because eliminating the influence is to the client's benefit, as the client will not receive poor work product from the financial planner.

False. Eliminating the influence of a conflict of interest is always to the benefit of a client, but the client may not see the benefit and may not agree to the change. In such a situation, the financial planner must remember that he or she has restored professional judgment to its rightful place in practice, maintaining his or her fiduciary duty to the client. If the client cannot be persuaded to see this benefit, the financial planner should consider the merits of continuing the engagement.

Suggestions on Practice Policy

Chapter 11

Conflicts of interest present two opportunities for financial planners. The first is the most important, the opportunity to demonstrate a high level of professional service to clients. The second opportunity is a result of the first, the opportunity to promote that level of service to prospective clients and the general marketplace. This chapter suggests that the best way to make the most of both opportunities is to develop a statement of policy and procedures about conflicts of interest to be used in a financial planning practice. A financial planner cannot be expected to be diligent about conflicts of interest without a clear statement about policy and resulting procedures to serve as a reference point.

The policy can be integrated into an existing code of ethics or can be a separate document. Of course the code of ethics for any certifying body that provides professional certification to the planner, such as the CFP Board, or professional association to which the planner belongs, such as the Financial Planning Association would serve as a frame of reference for the policy statement and procedures. First we will discuss what should be included in a statement of policy and procedures. Then we will consider how to promote the resulting level of professional service as a differentiating factor for the practice.

Policy and Procedures for the Practice

Developing an effective statement of policy and procedures for conflicts of interest requires an underlying commitment by the financial planner to succeed at three critical objectives:

1. Staying informed about conflicts of interest and the problems they cause when not addressed;
2. Maintaining sound professional judgment when faced with a conflict of interest;
3. Carrying out that judgment in all actions involving the conflict. This commitment will provide the motivation and direction for the statement.

The statement of policy should begin with a working definition of a conflict of interest. The definition should read something like this: *a conflict of interest as an interest the financial planner has that competes with the planner's interest in a client to the point of distorting the planner's professional judgment in service to that client.* The statement of policy should then proceed to describe the two general types of conflicts of interest, those interests outside and those interests inside of practice. Providing some of the typical subgroups of conflicts of interest originating outside and within practice would be useful. Finally, appropriate remedies for the general types of conflicts should be prescribed.

Procedures to Reveal Conflicts of Interest

When a definition and the types of conflicts of interest have been spelled out in a policy statement, procedures should be provided to *discover* conflicts of interest in the practice and state what practice personnel *should do* when a conflict of interest is suspected. The procedures to discover conflicts of interest should start with a few clear statements of *how* a financial planner can recognize a conflict of interest. The *before work product* indicator of impaired professional judgment is the preferred method to be described, because it saves difficulty for the client. The client does not have to be the recipient of poor work for the conflict of interest to be discovered.

The poor work product indicator is useful to discover past mistakes in the practice, to prevent the same mistake from occurring again. For this reason the poor work product method also should be described in the procedures, for use with completed cases, pending the next annual review.

When the descriptions of how to recognize a conflict of interest are in place, the financial planning practice should consider two regularly scheduled processes to screen for conflicts of interest. To prepare for the first process, financial planners in the practice should record any additional *relationships* or *ventures* held with a client in the client file as soon as the information is known. These cases can then be reviewed regularly to consider if a conflict of interest is present. The before work product (impaired professional judgment) criteria should be used for pending cases and cases in process, while the poor work product indicator (Does poor work product indicate a conflict of interest?) is more suitable for completed cases.

In the second process, completed cases with *no indication* of additional relationships or ventures can be randomly selected and reviewed on a regularly scheduled basis to assist in recognizing conflicts of interest that may have influenced work product in the past. When possible, the use of triangulation is a good idea for both scheduled procedures, using two lines of sight in addition to the viewpoint of the serving planner.

Procedure when a Conflict of Interest is Suspected.

When a conflict of interest is detected or suspected by a financial planner or other staff member, a procedure should be provided stating what should be done. This can be as simple as contacting the financial planner in the practice designated to manage conflicts of interest. If the practice has no appointed planner, the principal of the firm should be contacted. That individual can then proceed with assessing the information, making a decision regarding any conflict, and applying a remedy when appropriate. When professional resources are sufficient, triangulation will allow three individuals to consider the situation.

Financial planners and paraplanners in a firm continually should be encouraged to recognize conflicts of interest and speak with the appropriate planner charged with managing conflicts of interest. Staff members also should be trained to become familiar with conflicts of interest and encouraged to speak freely regarding concerns with the appropriate financial planner.

Promoting the Quality of Practice

This book has been about practice and not advertising a practice. However, high quality practice is something to be proud of and should be promoted to potential clients and the general public. As a closing thought, when promoting the quality of a financial planning practice, consider that all materials used to advertise the practice include a statement like this: *Sound professional judgment and work product are hallmarks of this firm.* To add seriousness to this claim, consider adding an additional comment such as: *Because of this, conflicts of interest are taken seriously and strongly discouraged.* This information could be placed on the firm website as well as in brochures describing the services of the practice.

Conflicts of interest are ironic. The problems they pose can become a means of positive distinction for the professional who recognizes and deals with them appropriately. Your position on conflicts of interest in practice can be seen as an important characteristic of quality practice to clients, other professionals, and the general public. Hopefully this book has contributed to your understanding of conflicts of interest and constructive ways to deal with them. The rest is up to you. Good luck!

References

Chapter 1

AICPA. (2009). *AICPA Code of Professional Conduct.* Retrieved June 19, 2009from http://tax.aicpa.org/Resources.

AICPA/PFS. (2009). *Statement on Responsibilities in Personal Financial Planning Practice.* Retrieved June 20, 2009 fromhttp://pfp.aicpa.org/Resources.

American Bar Association (2008). *Model Rules of Professional Conduct.* Retrieved June 19, 2009 from www.abanet.org.

Brandon, E. D., & Welch, H. O. (2009). *The history of financial planning: The transformation of financial services.* Hoboken, N. J.: John Wiley & Sons.

Calormiris, C., & Mason, J. (August 24, 2007). Reclaim power from the rating agencies. *Financial Times,* p. 11.

Certified Financial Planner Board of Standards, Inc. (2009). *CFP Board's Standards of Professional Conduct.* Retrieved December 27, 2009 from http://www.cfp.net/learn/codeofethics.asp.

Certified Financial Planner Board of Standards, Inc. (2009) Letter to House Committee on Financial Services, November 2, 2009. Retrieved December 27, 2009 from http://www.cfp.net/downloads/HR3817_Letter_2009-11-02.pdf.

Certified Financial Planner Board of Standards, Inc. (2009). *Public Policy and Advocacy,* para. 1-3. Retrieved December 27, 2009 from http://www.cfp.net/advocacy/coalition.asp.

Churchill, J. (2007). Surprise! FPA wins lawsuit against sec and the broker-dealer exemption. *Registered Rep,* para. 1. Retrieved December 27, 2009 from http://registeredrep.com/news/SEC_Broker_Dealer_Exemption/.

Coval, J., Jurek, J. & Stafford, E. (2009). The economics of structured finance. *Journal of Economic Perspectives, 23*(1), 3-25.

Crowe, R. (1993). Meeting client needs through financial planning. In R. M. Crowe, & C. E. Hughes (Eds.), *Fundaments of financial planning* (pp. 1- 28). Bryn Mawr, PA: The American College.

David, H., & Goldstein, M. (2007, June 18). This investment could turn ugly. *BusinessWeek,* Issue 4039, retrieved from EBSCOhost database June 19, 2009.

Financial Planning Association (2009). *Code of ethics.* Retrieved July 1, 2009 from http://www.fpaforfinancialplanning.org/AboutFPA/CodeofEthics/.

Financial Planning Association (2007). *Legal Challenge to SEC's Broker-Dealer Rule.* Retrieved April 6, 2007, from http://www.fpanet.org/member/govt_relation.

Financial Planning Association of Australia Limited (March 2, 2006). News and events. *FPA adopts Principles for Managing Conflicts of Interest.* Retrieved April 6, 2007, from www.fpa.asn.au/Home/News?FPA.

Flesher, D. L., Miranti, P. J., & Previts, G. J. (1996). The first century of the CPA. *Journal of Accountancy, 182*(4), 51-58.

Foote, C., Gerardi, K., & Willen, P. S. (2008). Negative equity and foreclosure: Theory and evidence. *Journal of Urban Economics, 64*(2): 234–245.

Gerardi, K., Lehnert, A., Sherlund, S. M., & Willen, P. Forthcoming. Making sense of the subprime crisis. *Brookings Papers on Economic Activity.*

Healy, J. (2009, June 4). As Deficits Mount, Fed Chief Calls for a Path to Fiscal Balance. *New York Times. Business/Financial Desk,* p. B3.

Hopewell, L. (1989). Conflicts of interest: A profession maturing. *Journal of Financial Planning, 2*(4), 163.

Jones, A. H. M. (1964). *The later Roman Empire, 284-602: A social, economic, and Administrative Survey, vol. 1.* Norman, OK: University of Oklahoma Press.

Kim, Y. (2008). Ratings and the Current Financial Crisis: A Modeling Perspective. *RMA Journal, 91(2), 48-53.*

Lengell, S. (2009, March 30). Bailout fund nearly spent; $135 billion remains of $700 billion TARP rescue. *Washington Times, p. A6.*

Levitt, A. (2007, September 7). Conflicts and the credit crunch. *The Wall Street Journal,* p. A15.

Mayer, C., Pence, K., & Sherlund, S. M. (2009). The rise in mortgage defaults. *Journal of Economic Perspectives, 23(1),* 27-50.

New Hampshire Securities Regulation (2005, July 12), Retrieved September 18, 2005 from http://www.sos.nh.gov/securities/PRESSR07_12_2005.pdf

Sherlund, S. (2008). The Past, present, and future of subprime mortgages. *Finance and Economics Discussion Series 2008-63,* Federal Reserve Board.

Simon, R. (Nov. 1992). The broken promise of financial planning [Section: Your Finances]. *Money, 21* (11), 132-143.

Society of Financial Service Professionals. (2008). *Code of Professional Responsibility.* Retrieved June 18, 2009 from www.financialpro.org.

Strier, F. (2008). Rating the raters: Conflicts of interest in the rating firms. *Business and Society Review, 113*, 533-553.

Suskie, L. (2009). Assessing student learning: A common sense guide. San Francisco, CA: Jossey-Bass.

The National Association of Personal Financial Advisors. (2009). *Code of Ethics.* Retrieved June 17, 2009 from www. napfa.org.

Thompson, A., Callahan, E., O'Toole, C., & Rajendra, G. (2007). Global CDO market: Overview and outlook. *Global Secularization and Structured Finance. Deutsche Bank, 8-14.*

Thompson, D. R. (2002). Financial planner DNA. *Journal of Financial Planning, 15*(7), 30-33.

Chapter 2

Certified Financial Planner Board of Standards, Inc. (2009). *CFP Board's Standards of Professional Conduct.* Retrieved March 11, 2010 from http://www.cfp.net/ Downloads/2008Standards.pdf.

Introduction to life insurance & annuities. (2009). Greenwood Village, CO: College for Financial Planning.

Leimberg, S. R., & Doyle, R. J. (2004). *Tools & techniques of life insurance planning.* Cincinnati, OH: The National Underwriter Company.

Miner, D. A., Wagner, W. J., Stenken, J. F., & King, S. E. (Eds.). (2009).*Tax facts on insurance & employee benefits.* (2009). Cincinnati, OH: The National Underwriter Company.

Chapter 3

Certified Financial Planner Board of Standards, Inc. (2009). *CFP Board's Standards of Professional Conduct.* Retrieved June 18, 2009 from http://www.cfp.net/ Downloads/2008Standards.pdf.

Fiduciary*360.* (2006). *Prudent practices for investment stewards.* Sewickley, PA: Author.

Chapter 4

ABA Code of Professional Responsibility, Ethical Consideration 5-1, 1969.

AICPA/PFS (2009). *Statement on Responsibilities in Personal Financial Planning Practice.* Retrieved June 20, 2009 from http://pfp.aicpa.org/Resources.

American Institute of Certified Public Accountants (2008). *AICPA Code of Professional Conduct,* Retrieved September 20, 2009 from www.aicpa.org/about/code/index.html.

American Medical Association (2009). *Code of Medical Ethics.* Retrieved September 20, 2009 from www.ama-assn.org.

American Psychological Association (2008). *Ethical Principles Of Psychologists And Code Of Conduct.* Retrieved September 20, 2009 from www.apa.org/ethics/code2002.html.

Black, H. C. (1971). *Black's law dictionary.* St. Paul, MN: West Publishing Company.

Certified Financial Planner Board of Standards (2009). *Code of ethics and professional responsibility.* Retrieved May 1, 2009 from www.cfp.net/certificants.conduct.asp

Davis, M. (2001). Introduction. In M. Davis & A. Stark (Eds.). *Conflict of interest in the professions* (pp.3-19). New York, NY: Oxford University Press.

Equitable Office Bldg. Corp., F. Supp. 531, District Court of New York, 1949.

Gray, J. A. (1994). Reforms to improve client protection and compensation against personal financial planners' unethical business practices. *American Business Law Journal 32*(2), 245-277.

Healy, J. (2009, June 4). As Deficits Mount, Fed Chief Calls for a Path to Fiscal Balance. *New York Times. Business/ Financial Desk,* p. B3.

Hodson, R. and Sullivan, T. 1990. *The social organization of work.* Belmont, CA: Wadsworth.

Huebner, S. S., & Black, K. (1982). *Life insurance* (10th ed.). Englewood Cliffs, NJ: Prentice-Hall.

McCall, D. M. (2004). Financial planners' growing professional liability. *Journal of Financial Services Professionals (58)*6, 57-67.

Moore, D. A., & Loewenstein, G. (2004). Self-interest, automaticity, and the psychology of conflict of interest. *Social Justice Research, (17)*2, 189-202.

Rattiner, J. H. (2006). Torn: The ethical dilemmas of your client's divorce. *Journal of Financial Planning (19)*4, 28-34.

Roos, P. A. (1992). Professions. In Reskin, B. F. & Borgatta, M. L. (Eds.), *The encyclopedia of sociology* (pp. 1552-1557). New York, NY: Macmillan.

Society Of Financial Service Professionals (2003). *Code of professional responsibility of the society of Financial Service Professionals.* Retrieved September 20, 2009 from www. financialpro.org.

Stein, J. M. (1971). *Random House dictionary of the English language.* New York, NY: Random House.

Vessenes, K. (1997). Avoiding lawsuits based on conflicts of interest. *Journal of Financial Planning (10)*6, 22-24.

Chapter 5

Davis, M. (2001). Introduction. In M. Davis & A. Stark (Eds.). *Conflict of interest in the professions* (pp. 3-19). New York, NY: Oxford University Press.

The dangers of distraction. (2009, March). *Harvard Management Update, 14*(3), 1-5.

Chapter 6

Davis, M. (2001). Introduction. In M. Davis & A. Stark (Eds.). *Conflict of interest in the professions* (pp.3-19). New York, NY: Oxford University Press.

Stark, A. (2001). Comparing conflict of interest across the professions. In M. Davis & A. Stark (Eds.). *Conflict of interest in the professions* (pp. 335-351). New York, NY: Oxford University Press.

Chapter 7

Bearden, F. C. (2001). Conflicts of interest in providing financial planning to friends, acquaintances and relatives. *Financial Counseling and Planning, 12*(1), 27-36.

Bearden, F. C. (2002). Conflicts of interest in financial planning practice. *Journal of Financial Planning, 15*(2), 86-91.

Stark, A. (2001). Comparing conflict of interest across the professions. In M. Davis & A. Stark (Eds.). *Conflict of interest in the professions* (pp. 335-351). New York, NY: Oxford University Press.

Chapter 8

Bearden, F. C. (2009). Conflicts of interest within a financial planning practice. In *2009 Financial Planning Perspectives Audio Series* [CD]. Greenwood Village, CO: College for Financial Planning.

Bigel, K. (1998). The correlations of professionalization and compensation sources with the ethical development of personal investment planners. *Financial Services Review, 7*(4), 223-237.

Bigel, K. (2000). The ethical orientation of financial planners who are engaged in investment activities: A comparison of United States practitioners based on professionalism and compensation sources. *Journal of Business Ethics, 28,* 323-337.

Cordell, D. M., & Lemoine, C. The elephant in the life insurance industry. *Journal of Financial Planning, 22*(5), 38-41.

Harrington, C. (2006, March 20-April 2). Advisor compensation tops conflict of interest fears. *Accounting Today, 16-17.*

Lins, G. (1998). "Soft dollars" and other brokerage arrangements. *Journal of Financial Planning, 11*(1), 89-92.

Stark, A. (2001). Comparing conflict of interest across the professions. In M. Davis & A. Stark (Eds.). *Conflict of interest in the professions* (pp. 335-351). New York, NY: Oxford University Press.

Tuohy, L. (2006, March 23). All planners should be fee-based. *Money Management*, p. 4.

Vessenes, K. (1997). Avoiding lawsuits based on conflicts of interest. *Journal of Financial Planning (10)*6, 22-24.

Chapter 9

Berg, B. L. (1998). *Qualitative research methods for the social sciences* (3rd ed.). Boston, MA: Allyn and Bacon.

Creswell, J. W. (19988). *Qualitative inquire and research design: Choosing among five traditions.* Thousand Oaks, CA: SAGE Publications.

Davis, M. (2001). Introduction. In M. Davis & A. Stark (Eds.). *Conflict of Interest in the professions.* New York, NY: Oxford University Press.

Festinger, L. (1957). *A theory of cognitive dissonance.* Evanston, IL: Row, Peterson, and Company.

Chapter 10

Lynch, J. T. (2009). Financial service professionals earn their compensation. *Journal of Financial Service Professionals, 63*(4), 27-29.

Stark, A. (2001). Comparing conflict of interest across the professions. In M. Davis & A. Stark (Eds.). *Conflict of Interest in the professions.* New York, NY: Oxford

Index

Page number in bold refer to references.